Amazing You
Enjoy the Power to
Get It Done, Get Stronger, Get Credit for It ...
featuring Secrets of Extreme Confidence

from GetTheBigYES.com

Tom Marcoux

Spoken Word Strategist

Executive Coach – Pitch Coach

Speaker-Author of 43 books

CEO

A QuickBreakthrough Publishing Edition

Copyright © 2017 Tom Marcoux Media, LLC
ISBN: 0997809868
ISBN-13: 978-0997809862

All rights reserved. No part of this book may be reproduced or transmitted in any form by any means electronic or mechanical, including photocopying, recording or by any information storage and retrieval system without written permission from the publisher.

QuickBreakthrough Publishing is an imprint of Tom Marcoux Media, LLC. More copies are available from the publisher, Tom Marcoux Media, LLC. Please write TomSuperCoach@gmail.com

or visit Tom's blogs: www.YourBodySoulandProsperity.com
PitchPowerFest.com   InstaMaxPro.com

This book was developed and written with care. Names and details were modified to respect privacy.

Notice: Copyrights for guest articles remain with the guest authors. Fair Use is related to commentary, news reporting, research, and scholarship.

Disclaimer: The author and publisher acknowledge that each person's situation is unique, and that readers have full responsibility to seek consultations with health, financial, spiritual and legal professionals. The author and publisher make no representations or warranties of any kind, and the author and publisher shall not be liable for any special, consequential or exemplary damages resulting, in whole or in part, from the reader's use of, or reliance upon, this material.:

Other Books by Tom Marcoux:
- Soar with Confidence: Pitch – Lead – Succeed
- Dark Arts Defense Against Toxic People
- Darkest Secrets of Charisma
- What the Rich Don't Say about Getting Rich
- Secrets of Awesome Dinner Guests: Walt Disney, Steve Jobs …
- Soar! Nothing Can Stop You This Year
- Time Management Secrets the Rich Won't Tell You
- Darkest Secrets of Persuasion and Seduction Masters
- Darkest Secrets of Making a Pitch to the Film / TV Industry

Praise for *Amazing You: Get It Done! Get Stronger, Get Credit for It* and Tom Marcoux

• "Tom Marcoux cuts through the myths and provides you with powerful methods to take your life to a higher level. More done in less time."
– David Barron, founder of New Hampshire Hypnosis, NewHampshireHypnosis.com

• "In his work, Tom Marcoux shows you how to be a better communicator, to get people to actually listen to you and believe you, and then act on what you say." – Danek S. Kaus, co-author, *Power Persuasion*

Praise for Tom Marcoux's Other Work:

• "Concerned about networking situations? Get *Relax Your Way Networking*. Success is built on high trust relationships. Master Coach Tom Marcoux reveals secrets to increase your influence."
– Greg S. Reid, Author, *Think and Grow Rich Series*

• "In Tom Marcoux's *Now You See Me*, the powerful and easy-to-use ideas can make a big difference in your business and your personal relationships." – Allen Klein, author of *You Can't Ruin My Day*

• "In *Darkest Secrets of Persuasion and Seduction Masters: How to Protect Yourself and Turn the Power to Good*, learn useful countermeasures to protect you from being darkly manipulated."
– David Barron, co-author, *Power Persuasion*

• "In *Connect*, Tom's advice on how to remain true to yourself and establish authentic rapport with clients is both insightful and reality based. He [shows how] to establish oneself as a credible expert."
- Arthur P. Ciaramicoli, Ed.D., Ph.D., author *The Curse of the Capable*

• "In *Reduce Clutter, Enlarge Your Life*, Marcoux will help you get rid of the physical and mental clutter occupying precious space in your life. You'll reclaim wasted energy, lower your stress, and find time for new opportunities." – Laura Stack, author of *Execution IS the Strategy*

Visit Tom's blogs: InstaMaxPro.com   PitchPowerFest.com
YourBodySoulandProsperity.com

Tom Marcoux

CONTENTS*

*These are highlights. Much more is in this book!

Dedication, Acknowledgments, Free eBook, more	6
Book 1: Get It Done, Get Stronger, Get Credit for It	7
Time Leverage (Better than Time Management)	10
Get Credit for It Is About Telling a Story	21
Answers to Specific Time Management Questions	33
The 9-Minute Miracle to Unleash the Amazing You	39
Book 2: Get Stronger (Quiet Down Feelings of Being Overwhelmed)	55
Bonus Material	97
Don't Let Fear Kill Your Divine Appointment	113
Stop Blocking the Amazing You	129
Final Word; Excerpt from *Darkest Secrets of Persuasion and Seduction Masters: How to Protect Yourself and Turn the Power to Good*	147,148
Special Offer Just for Readers, About the Author Tom Marcoux, Spoken Word Strategist & Executive Coach	147,154

DEDICATION AND ACKNOWLEDGEMENTS

This work is dedicated to YOU. Here are **Special Offers:**

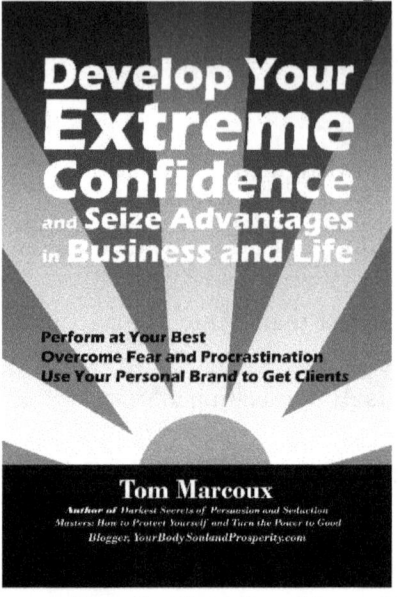

- **Get your free eBook** *Develop Your Extreme Confidence and Seize Advantages in Business and Life* at http://bit.ly/29bVpox
- Apply for a **Free Consultation** with Tom Marcoux https://tomsupercoach.com/breakthrough/

This book also dedicated to the terrific book/film consultant, and author Johanna E. Mac Leod. Thanks to Barry Adamson II for editing some sections. Thanks to Johanna E. Mac Leod for this book's cover. Thanks to Diane Pascual for consulting on the cover. Thanks to my father, Al Marcoux, for his concern and efforts for me ... and to my mother, Sumiyo Marcoux, a kind, generous soul. Thank you to Higher Power ... and to our readers, audiences, clients, my graduate students and my team members of Tom Marcoux Media, LLC and GetTheBigYES.com. The best to you.

Book 1
Get It Done! Get Stronger, Get Credit for It

"Streetlamps hardly make a dent in the darkness. It's after 9 pm. Telegraph Hill neighborhood, San Francisco. I had no idea that my life would be on the line," I began. *The audience clung to my words.*

"Here's how it began. I'm walking with the love of my life, Johanna.

How do I know that? I'll tell you. It's 17 years later, and she's here in this audience.

Johanna and I are walking—when one block away, we hear CRASH. We see a huge Ford F-150 truck that slams into Johanna's *parked*, little Toyota truck.

This huge truck pulls back and smashes her truck again.

I go 'knight in shining armor' because I'm concerned for Johanna. Because she's going to be hit by an emotional piano because it's *not* her truck. It's her *parents'* truck. She'll be hit by "What did you do?! How did you let this hit and run thing happen?!"

"So, I'm running down the street. She walks down the sidewalk because *she's* sane and rational.

"That guy turns his truck, trying to get away, and PTAK!—hits me, right in the chest.

"I don't know how bad it is. I'm full of adrenaline.

"He keeps pushing me with his huge truck. I can't get away. He's already hit me. He might run me over. So, I hold onto the hood; my feet are off the street.

"What would you do?"

[The audience members pause. A number of them look baffled.]

"Fortunately, we're here talking about how to make great decisions and make your life better.

"We're focused on *Get It Done, Get Stronger and Get Credit for it.*"

* * *

That's the beginning of one of my signature speeches.

Why did I begin with a story of how I tried to protect my sweetheart's feelings by risking my life?

I learned how emotions can run how we make decisions.

My friend, how are things going in your life? Have you fallen into default settings?

Are you making good choices?

I am NOT saying that taking on a F-150 truck was a good idea. I would *not* do it again.

In fact, I ended up at the Emergency room.

A doctor pressed on my chest.

"Does this hurt?" he said.

"Yeah."

"Does this hurt?"

"Yeah."

"Does this hurt?"

"Stop that!"

The truck in your life may not be an actual F-150 truck. But if you feel stressed out all the time, you're being impacted. *There's some kind of truck in your life.*

If on Sunday night, you're dreading Monday morning, *there's some kind of truck in your life.*

Through this book, I'll be your Executive Coach. I'll help you get stuff out of your way so you create what you want in life. I'll provide client-tested, research-based methods so you'll overcome procrastination.

We'll make sure you *get stronger* so you can *Get It Done!* Also, we'll identify how you can *Get Credit for It!*

All three elements are crucial so you rise to a higher level of success and happiness.

Think about it. If you get it done, but you're a physical wreck—you lose.

If you get things done, but you don't *Get Credit for It*—you cannot get new clients. And, you'll lose your current clients—if they don't know, in their gut, how their lives are better because you've brought them significant benefits.

I've got a secret for you: You can *unleash the Amazing You!*

Some might say that's overstating things.

I know from years of working with thousands of clients, audience members, MBA students and more, that **we can rise to the *Amazing! Level.***

Let's Open the Door to the *Amazing YOU*

What do you want to do that, at this moment, feels like a big stretch? You might even say that if you accomplish that big dream, it would be amazing.

I've helped clients write books, give award-winning speeches, become filmmakers, lead companies and more. All of that was Amazing!

When a new client begins with me, I say, **"You will achieve more than you believe."** As an Executive Coach and the Spoken Word Strategist, I help the person express their Best Self.

Here's something that I've learned about Amazing! We don't do *Amazing!* alone.

My phrase is *Amazing happens with Alliances.*

In this book, I am aligning with you. I'll show you how to connect with people—so they know you, like you, and trust you.

I call myself an OptiRealist. I'm optimistic that we can do better. With my own mentors, coaches and training, I've risen from a terribly shy, timid boy to directing feature films, speaking in front of audiences of 700 people and more.

Not bad for an introvert. I've learned how to drop certain actions connected with being perceived as shy.

If you're not sure if you're an introvert … If someone says, "Party," and you ask, "How long is it?"—"When can I leave?" … You're an introvert!

An introvert *pays energy* when they're around people. On the other hand, extroverts soak up the energy when they're in a crowd.

Introverts need to rev up before an event, recover energy during the event—and recharge their personal battery with alone-time after the event.

I mentioned that I'm an OptiRealist. **I'm realistic** that we need to *use systems to Get It Done!*

Let's get into action now.

We're focusing on something better than time management; I call it *Time Leverage.*

Handle Fear and Create Your Better Life

"Tell me something I need to know about handling fear," my client, Ted, said.

"Based on our conversation so far, I have a powerful process that can help you take your business to a higher level. For many of us, fear is subtle. It's beneath the surface. We just seem too busy to do certain things. For example, how are your marketing calls going?"

"They are not going. I just can't make time for them," Ted said.

"I hear you. When I started my first business, I called myself a 'little fire truck.' Putting out fires here and there. But I was stuck in a rut. I later realized (through good coaching) that I was letting fear hold me back," I said.

"How?"

"I was afraid of **disappointment**. I was afraid of disappointing my sweetheart. I was afraid of disappointing myself. So, what did I do? It was more about what I did NOT do. To rise to another level, you need to do things that make you uncomfortable. Things that are outside your comfort zone. Many people just ignore the whole thing. For example, they do not have specific goals about making marketing phone calls. I've learned this truth: *What you dread, gets you ahead,*" I said.

"Let's work on this together," I continued. "To release you from hesitation caused by fear, we're going to talk about *Setting Goals on 3 Levels: Good, Excellent and Amazing!* So, in one day, what would be an *Amazing!* number of marketing phone calls for you to make?"

"Eighteen."

"So that's *Amazing!* What would be a 'good' number of calls?"

"Six."

"Are you sure you could make six calls during the day?"

"I'm not sure."

"How about two phone calls?" I asked.

"Two? Sure, I could do that," Ted said.

"Good to hear. So, 'two phone calls' is at your 'Good' level," I said.

"I'm not sure that two is *Good*," Ted said.

"Two is **better than zero**," I said.

Ted smiled. "Yeah. You're right."

"Here's the helpful detail. Anything over 2 phone calls is on the 'Excellent' Level." This is how you can have Excellent Days."

* * *

Here's a special note: When you set the action to achieve "Good" at a modest level, you avoid disappointing yourself! That's important. Why? Many of us naturally tend to avoid what hurts. **Self-Disappointment hurts a lot.** Many of us are, subconsciously, making lots of efforts to avoid such pain.

Let's face it. Many of us hold great fear about disappointment. So, we live a lesser life. No more of that!

Use this *process of Good-Excellent-Amazing!* to get out of a rut.

Working with clients, I note that each client can become stronger to handle what I call the External Factor Disappointment. Sure, it hurts when a prospective client says a final and firm 'No.' One solution is to get in front of additional, high quality, prospective clients. I said to a team member:

"*If you hear 'No' from one and you only have one—it's a tragedy.*

If you hear 'No' and you have twenty to go, 'No' is just a step."

In summary:

Set your goals on the Good – Excellent – Amazing! Levels

Acknowledge when subconscious fear may be slowing you down.

Become skilled at taking action and remember: "Better than Zero!"

Realize that setting goals on the Amazing! Level is a process to expand your thinking.

The process of Good, Excellent and Amazing! is a system. It works for my clients. I use it.

Some days, I tell myself: One more phone call, that will be *Good!*

I like the days when I cross into *Excellent!*

In the recent three days, my editor and I completed 9 videos for my online class *"Get the Big YES: Use Extreme Confidence to Get Clients and Get It Done!"*

With my team member's help, I crossed over to Amazing!

Amazing! happens more often when you **write down your Amazing! Goals.**

Do you see how this relates to **Unleashing the Amazing YOU?**

Excellent.

How many of us have written things into a to-do list?

Then, stuff did *not* get done.

It just got pushed over to the next day, and the next day, and the next day.

To-do lists are *not powerful enough* for you to get it done, get stronger and get credit for it.

What we need is: **Time-Leverage.**

That's my term for *using systems so we get the most important things done.* Leverage is small efforts and BIG results.

We'll begin with the system called "N.O.W."

My friend, Thomas Price said, **"Source the audience's pain points."**

So, I'll ask you:

What's not working with your time management?

Are you procrastinating?

Many of us note that the To-Do List is a To-Don't List.

Can you relate to a To-Do List as a GUILT List?

It's time to do two things simultaneously Get Things Done and Get Stronger. To do that we use the N.O.W. process:

N – Nurture
O – Optimize
W – Work it

1. Nurture

"Nurture" may not be the first word you think of related to *Get It Done*. Still, it makes sense when we realize that we must have the energy to take action and complete tasks.

Here's a problem. Many of us drain our own energy. How? It's the way we "keep score." We're keeping score of the negative things in our life. It's as if we're subscribing to a **myth** that one can punish oneself to improve.

When it comes to time management, many of us tend to focus on what we've failed to do. That causes us pain, and it's the opposite of "nurture."

For example, my new client Sarah, 35, was working a "safe local government job." But her heart was calling her to be a speaker and a business coach.

She kept track by concentrating on all of the things she did NOT complete. She was upset with herself for failing to write her new speech. Before she worked with me, Sarah repeatedly put herself down for failing to consistently rehearse.

"I feel overwhelmed," Sarah told me.

An Important Part of Solving the "Feeling Overwhelmed" Problem

Have you noticed yourself or a friend focusing on list writing as the primary part of time management?

How's that working?

Many of us write a list and procrastinate on certain tasks. Here's an important point. The list is too long and it's not prioritized.

Instead, we focus on **Top Six Targets**—these are the crucial tasks you must get done on the next day of your life.

When we focus on Top Six Targets, we separate ourselves from looking at a long To-Do List with 30 tasks we failed to complete.

Here's how you do "Top Six Targets."

Just before you go to sleep at night, take about one minute and write down your *Top Six Targets* for your next day. I write them on a 3x5 card.

I share with audiences: "2 for you, 2 for family, 2 for work."

Then the next day, you wake up and you do **"Worst First."** That is, you do the most important thing first.

I've noticed a paradox. The thing you don't feel like doing will do the most for your career. My phrase is: *What you dread, gets you ahead.*

You do that which is most important (the *Worst First*)—early in the day.

If you take care of these Top Six Targets, you will have a

good **day.**

For me, exercise every day is a Top Six Target.

The Top Six Targets help you avoid losing time by not knowing what to do when you start your new day.

My audiences tell me that they like the topic "Add one hour of High Productivity to your day." Top Six Targets ties directly into that.

The Top Six Targets are like marching orders. You know where to start in your next day. You get straight to work on what's most important. This helps you add that High Productivity Hour each day.

The mentors and the successful people I've learned from, have shared that they give themselves marching orders before the next day. They know what they're up to. They know what's moving them forward.

When I was in college, I would go to sleep sad. I did not have the Top Six Targets.

For years (after graduating), I write down my Top Six Targets. I find my focus, and I avoid feeling overwhelmed.

In college, I did ***not*** nurture myself and my own strength. Instead, I kept score of how I was not measuring up to some fictional ideal in my own mind.

Have you noticed that many of us are keeping score in a way that makes us hurt?

Why? It's just natural for us to focus on negative details.

Blame it on our ancestors. It's our ancestors who noticed: "Hey, that's a saber-toothed tiger. That is negative." Those are the ancestors who lived.

The other ones who said, "Hello, kitty." Those are the ones who died and could *not* pass on their genes.

Some years ago, I wrote this phrase: **Keep Score and Achieve More.**

The vital distinction is you'll do better by **using a system** to *keep score of what is positive and empowering in your daily life.*

If you're only keeping score of negative things like what you're procrastinating on, you'll drain your own energy.

Instead, we'll focus on a way to solve procrastination.

An Important Part of Solving Procrastination (Preset the Trigger Sequence)

My client Andrew, a teacher, wanted to write a book.

He told me: "I don't have the willpower. If only, I could get motivated."

I said, "Do you do cardio at the gym?"

"Yeah…"

"You could place a notepad on the stand part of the treadmill, where people put a book to read."

"Okay."

"And you could jot down any ideas you have for dialogue. Or for the first sentence of a chapter. Or a last sentence of a chapter."

"It's possible," Andrew said.

"The notepad would serve as *a Trigger* so that you'd do some writing every day."

I call this process ***Preset the Trigger Sequence.***

With another client, Mark, I helped him take care of his problem about sending out invoices. I said, "Use the act of hanging up the phone after talking with a client as *a Trigger* to immediately send out the follow-up email with the invoice. No hesitation. Just make this automatic. Do not take a break. Just do it immediately."

As I mentioned earlier: *What you dread, gets you ahead.*

The solution is to set up a System. No hesitation. Make the choice once and this is part of how you Preset the Trigger Sequence.

I emphasize that we Preset a Trigger Sequence by making a good choice when the situation is "cool."

Then, when the situation is "hot," we automatically take positive action.

2. Optimize

When I say "Optimize," I refer to "Optimize Your Goals."

My client, Pat, 51, was transitioning from doing corporate work as a project manager to his new work with his own company.

"I just don't know how to sell," Pat told me.

"We've covered a number of processes related to selling — and even better, for you to enroll clients in what you're offering. I'm curious. How are your marketing phone call going?"

"I'm just not getting them done."

"Okay. What would you call a good number of calls?"

"If I did one phone call a day, that would be good," Pat said with a dash of cynicism in his vocal tone.

"Good is **better than zero**," I replied. "Here's something helpful. We'll use 3 Levels of Goals: *Good, Excellent and Amazing!*"

I explained that it's powerful when we make each day into a "good day." That is, you set a modest goal — plus you expand your thinking with two other levels."

"Pat, if you do one phone call that's Good. What would be amazing?" I asked.

"9 calls."

"I'm with you. So, one phone call is Good. 9 phone calls are Amazing. And anything over 1 phone call is *Excellent*. You can now strive to have Excellent days."

This was a turning point for Pat.

Here's my question for you:

How can you apply this process of setting goals on the 3 Levels of Good, Excellent, Amazing!?

3. Work It

I first shared this in an article I wrote entitled *Make Your Brand Irresistible – Get Clients! ...*

"If only the people I meet could really understand the value I bring to my clients," my new client Sandra said, deep concern in her eyes.

"I'm right there with you. I'll take you through a process; I call it **'Work it and trim it,'**" I began. "We're talking about using **Story** and making things **Brief** and **Compelling**."

a) *Story*

Novice business owners give people a list of what they do. Or they use an Elevator Speech that sounds like a commercial. **These things break rapport.** Instead, I guide my own clients to have a menu of stories that they can share. The story is what creates connection, and the story moves emotions.

Here's an example:

Wendy: "I'm curious. Do you have your own company or do you work as part of a team?"

Cheryl: "I have my own company. We sell children's apparel online."

Wendy: "What inspired you to do that?"

Cheryl: (talks about how she was inspired by her three-year-old son).

Wendy: "Wow. You light up as you tell me all about that."

Cheryl: "Yeah. I still want to know what you do."

Wendy: "I help business owners like you invite people into their website. Recently, I helped a client, Irina, create a whole new homepage that gets people to click and dive into her website. She's now capturing many more new visitors. The improvement is 237%."

The above example is part of what I call an Elevator Dialogue.

My point is: Tell a well-crafted story. Make the emotional connection.

b) Brief

How do you know if what you're saying is brief enough?

Find out if the person can say it back to you.

Seven days ago, I got a phone call. "Tom, I think you'd be good to facilitate a marketing meeting at the company I work at. You *are* the Spoken Word Strategist."

Boom! My marketing was working.

Some time ago, I made the mistake of having a bunch of words under my name on my business card, including "CEO, Executive Coach, Author of 43 books ..."

One of my own coaches pushed me. He said, "Why are you doing that?"

I replied, "I want to show that I'm different."

"Yeah, you're different. *But what counts is that people remember you*," he said.

Many talented people find it hard to zero-in on the one thing that makes them great and different.

Ultimately, I learned that you keep testing things. When people can say something back to you, when they remember it, your marketing is working.

More does not mean better. Memorable is better.

c) Compelling

What is the pain that you alleviate for the client?

Where do they hurt?

Turn that into a Story of how you've helped a previous client. That's compelling.

One of my clients said this:

"Tom Marcoux helped me get more done in 10 days than other coaches in 2 years." – Brad Carlson, CEO, Mindstrong, LLC.

I've worked with CEOs and other business leaders. Where's the pain? Wasting time or other resources.

So, I help clients use leverage—small effort for BIG results

* * *

Work It is part of *"Get Credit for It."*

For example, if your client does *not* know how their life has improved through working with you, you lose that client.

If you have clients that work with you for six months, and you want that client to sign up for six *more* months, you've "got to get credit for it."

For example, for one of my clients, I wrote a list of 20 things that my client had accomplished in a couple of months of working with me—as his Executive Coach.

This was eye-opening for my client. He was so pleased!

To "get credit for it" is about telling a story.

Tell the story and include *a quote from someone praising you*.

That's how you get credit. **You end your story with a quote from a happy client.**

Here's an example. In a job interview, a standard question is: "Tell me about your strength." You end your story with: "And that's when my supervisor Susan said, 'George, I can always count on you to come up with a solution that saves my company money.'"

That's how we get credit.

To continue with "work it," anytime someone praises you

for anything, make sure you hold onto the material. Save the emails. Print them out. Put them in a folder.

The process is to Work It. Here's another example. My new client, Amanda, came to me and said, "I'm confused. I can't go forward because I don't have clarity."

I responded, "I hear you. It would be great to travel this road"—I drew a vertical line on a sheet of paper—"a mystical road that has clarity and certainty. I've learned that the universe does NOT always give us that particular road. But there is another road. On this road, we rise to higher levels of success and happiness."

I drew a second vertical line showing a road veering to the right. I said, "On this road to the right ... you have a path that includes Motion and Discovery."

Motion and Discovery are parts of an adventure.

I said to Amanda, "I'm with you. As you try new things, you will have this experience. **Motion Brings Clarity."**

That's part of what I'm emphasizing with *Work it*. Try new things. Take appropriate risks. This is how you unleash the Amazing You.

Additional Material to Help You "Get It Done"...

Part Two of "Nurture":

Use Your Daily Journal of Victories and Blessings

Here's something even more powerful than *Top Six Targets*. It's your *Daily Journal of Victories and Blessings*.

This is NOT your day planner. This is separate.

The process of your Daily Journal of Victories and Blessings only takes two minutes—just before you go to sleep.

This is the antidote to being sad just before you go to sleep.

At the end of your day, you write down Your Victories in your Daily Journal. **Victories are things you accomplished.** I always write down my exercise because that is a personal victory for me.

On my page for the day (of my Daily Journal), I draw a box labelled *fun*. I want to have some fun each day. Don't you? I write down the fun moments of the day into a square I draw (a *Box for Fun).* For example, I had some fun when talking with a friend and later, viewing an episode of a TV program. I use Netflix on occasion. I saw a show that made me laugh — which I noted in my *Box for Fun.*

I invite you to write down your Victories and Blessings. A blessing could be a surprise phone call from a friend that you really enjoy.

If you implement Top Six Targets and Daily Journal of Victories and Blessings, you will feel better. You will go to sleep happy.

Another benefit: When you write down your Top Six Targets, you clear out your mind. You won't have to worry about remembering something vital for the next day.

If you don't clear out your mind, you can have trouble like I had when I flew to Boston — years ago. I flew from San Jose, California to Boston. I had the reels of my feature film. (That's when we used to use film.) I was supposed to go to a particular lab in the morning.

The problem was: I was not certain about my alarm clock. So, I lost a lot of sleep that night. Now, I'd have TWO alarm clocks.

My point is that it's wise to use better and better strategy. We focus on *Nurture and Keep Score.*

We focus on keeping score in a wise, uplifting and empowering way.

The phrase is: *Keep Score and Achieve More.*

Part Two of "Optimize Goals"
Three Forms of Goals:
- Golden Pull Goals
- Dark Boot Goals
- Green Goals

When I ask an audience: "What bothers you about setting goals?" I hear:
- "What if I set the wrong goal?"
- "What if I don't accomplish my goal?"

I have been concerned about both issues, and we'll talk about solutions related to both tough situations.

When I talk about *Optimizing Your Goals*, I'm concerned that we free ourselves from debilitating myths.

One myth is that it's possible that we only focus on the positive and still, we'll create what we want in life.

On the other hand, researchers note that many of us are *wired to focus more on the negative.*

I'm focused on what works.

While I was earning my degree in psychology, I was enchanted with the idea of just focusing on the positive stuff. One branch of psychology is called positive psychology. I wanted to focus only on positive psychology.

But in the real world, I realized what gets us to really get things done.

I don't know anyone when April 15th comes along, who says, "I love April 15th. I love giving my money to the government."

Why do we do taxes paperwork? To avoid tax penalties—

a negative consequence. This relates to what I call a *Dark Boot Goal* …

Three Forms of Goals – *The Goals Triangle*

Think of goals as a triangle. At the top of the triangle is the stuff we like to talk about: I call them *Golden Pull Goals*. They pull you forward.

But "avoid tax penalties" is a *Dark Boot Goal*. Think of it as the bottom-left point of the triangle. You do the work because you're being kicked in the rear by a Dark Boot.

At the right-side point of the triangle, we note "Green Goals."

- *Golden Pull Goals* are what we like to talk about.
- *Dark Boot Goals* are what get us to break procrastination.
- *Green Goals* renew our energy and bring some calm and peace into our life.

First, let me make this relevant to a question asked in my workshops: *"What if I set the wrong goal?"*

Connected to that concern is: "Are you setting *goals that stand together?"*

I'll share an example:

Let's say you start with a *Golden Pull Goal:* "Add $200,000 to the bottom-line for my business."

That goal can work when you add these goals:
- Make marketing phone calls *(Dark Boot Goal)*
- Walk one hour each day with my spouse *(Green Goal)*
- Do a brief meditation session upon awakening in the morning *(Green Goal)*

When you use the Three Forms of Goals (Golden Pull, Dark Boot, Green), **you can recover more easily from** working on a wrong goal.

If a goal is wrong for you, it could eat up your time and your energy. **Green Goals help you recover your energy.**

Without the Three Forms of Goals (Golden Pull, Dark Boot, and Green), you create a house of cards that cannot stand.

I realized this and this phrase rose in my thoughts:

"I noticed holes in how we set goals."

To replace, such "holes," you *create a sustainable pattern of goals.* You have all Three Forms (Golden Pull, Dark Boot, and Green).

Green Goals are vital. We need you to stay strong. That's why I title my speech "Get It Done! Get Stronger, Get Credit for It."

I emphasize if you get it done, but you're a physical wreck, you lose.

To get stronger, we take action for Green Goals.

When you have all Three Forms of Goals, you have more latitude to make errors. **At first glance, every high performer has pursued "wrong goals."** Steve Jobs led a team to make the Lisa computer. Presently, many people have never heard of the Lisa computer. Jobs said, "It was a great machine; we just couldn't sell any."

The excellent plan is to have a good base built upon your Green Goals (good nutrition, enough sleep, appropriate exercise, quiet time/prayer time and more).

"Build a superreserve in every area: have more than enough."
— Thomas Leonard

How We Use Strategy to Handle the Concern: "What if I don't accomplish the goal?"

As I mentioned, it's valuable to develop your *Goals*

Triangle. The Golden Pull Goal is your vision. That's what pulls you forward. We talked about the Dark Boot Goal that kicks your forward. That's usually related to stopping pain or avoiding pain.

So, what do you do about Dark Boot Goals?

When I first needed to do marketing phone calls, that was a Dark Boot Goal. I'd rather do anything else. Write a book. Give a speech. Walk 20 miles. You name it!

I knew I needed to set a quota of how many phone calls to place each day. But I was afraid. I was afraid of failing and disappointing myself or even feeling some shame when telling my sweetheart about failing to hit my goal.

That's when a phrase rose in my mind: **"Avoid ramming your head into the Wall of Disappointment."** By this I meant, that if I set a goal and failed, I'd feel great pain.

Then I came up with a useable strategy.

I call it: **3 Levels of Goals: Good, Excellent, Amazing!**

[I shared such details earlier in this book.]

I could start with a modest goal: 2 phone calls (with related follow-up emails). That would be Good. I could do that!

Anything over 2 phone calls (plus 2 emails) would be Excellent. 6 phone calls would be Amazing!

Two things go well with setting 3 Levels of Goals.

First, you are less likely to disappoint yourself because you CAN accomplish the modest goal at the "Good" level.

Second, you still set goals that stretch you. Better yet, you can SEE the goals that stretch you.

Here's an example:
Good: 2 phone calls
Excellent: 3 and over
Amazing!: 10 phone calls for the day.

By the way, in the above example: Two phone calls would be "Better than zero."

Use Dark Boot Goals to Strengthen Yourself

Although we like to talk about Golden Pull Goals, many of us are wired to react to Dark Boot Goals. Here's a powerful example. Some decades ago, there was a woman; we'll call her Sandra. She got married, and one day she goes to her husband and said, "I need $10." He said, "What for?"

She thought: "That's it. I'm never asking this man for $10 again in my life." She went out and went to work. She ultimately earned a position as a well-paid executive. She never had to worry about money ever again. She never had to go to her husband for money.

Now, that's a Dark Boot Goal. You don't want to be humiliated by having to ask someone for money. You want to control your life about money. Such a Dark Boot Goal works. It certainly worked for Sandra.

I always remember this story.

Strengthen Yourself with Green Goals

I named the Green Goal as something like a green forest—full of life. Healthy. We're talking about reducing "feeling overwhelmed." We want you to be strong and capable. Remember it's *Get It Done, Get Stronger, and Get Credit for It*.

To be stronger, set your Green Goals. They include exercise, nutrition, and quiet time. I meditate every morning. One top teacher of meditation was asked, "How long do you meditate every day?"

He said, "Three minutes."

I said, "I could do that!"

Every day, I meditate and check it off the list. I remember to *Keep Score and Achieve More*.

Use a Progress Log.

If you have a big report for work, keep a Progress Log. Let's say the report will be 5,000 words.

Did you write 25 words today? Write that down on your Progress Log.

25 words done. Great. That's **Better Than Zero.**

So, we have talked about the *Triangle of Goals.*

At the top: *Golden Pull Goals.* That's the vision stuff. Some people talk about "I want to enhance my company and add $200,000 to the bottom line."

What is the *Dark Boot Goal?* Here's an example: *I don't want to feel ashamed in front of my family that I'm not making progress.* If that's really what's going to push you forward then *do something about it every day.*

For example, I rehearse my speeches every day. Even just 9 minutes. If you rehearse 9 minutes in the morning, your subconscious mind will work on your speech all day long. This is a method I share with my clients.

Finally, we'll cover an example of a *Green Goal.*

We learn to *Stop, Breathe and Observe.*

Some years ago, my sweetheart and I went snorkeling in the Bahamas.

Here's how I share this story with my workshop audience:

"It's 90 degrees. You'd think that the water would be warm.

But it was relatively cold.

I learned two things happen in cold water.

What's worse that a cramp in your right leg?

[Audience members say, "Cramp in both legs."]

You're right there with me ... a cramp in both legs.

So, my sweetheart has to pull me in—to the shore.

It feels like half a mile. And I'm helping her by swimming with my arms. My legs don't work, and I'm using my arms.

We get back to the cruise ship, and I learn the second thing that happens in cold water.

Things shrink. ….

[Audience members laugh.]

My hand shrank. My wedding ring was lost in hundreds of yards of sand and water.

You ever lose something and you want to throw up. Blech!

Now this is something that can break a vacation.

But no.

I made sure to *Stop. Breathe. And Observe.*

We're still on vacation. I'm alive. My sweetheart is alive. We're in love.

The world is okay.

Let's try that now. *Stop.* Everyone now breathe in.

Hold it for a moment. … And breathe out.

Let's do it again.

Breathe in deeply. Let your abdomen expand.… And breathe out.

Good.

So, I did it. *Stop. Breathe. Observe.*

And I observed: We're on the Disney Cruise.

I call Guest Services. On the next day, I walk up to the person at Guest Services. It's a different person than the one on the phone.

I say, "I lost my wedding ring."

"Where did you lose it, sir?"

"If I knew where I lost it, would I be talking to you?" (I didn't say that out loud. But I was thinking it!)

I said, "I don't know. It's your island."

That's right. Disney not only owns Lucasfilm, Pixar and Marvel Studios.

They own an island.

I said, "It's your island. I was on your tram. I went to the lagoon."

"The lagoon." And the guy holds out a piece of paper. And connected to the paper was *my ring*.

This ring! *[I hold up my hand and show my wedding ring.]*

I learned that a married couple—a man and his wife—found the ring. I pictured that he saw it on the sand and said, "Oh! He's in trouble now!"

[Audience members laugh.]

I've shared with you: *Stop. Breathe. Observe.* Practice that. Make it a Green Goal for even just 3 minutes a day. Some people call this meditation. Take the time to sit still. Stop. Breathe. Observe.

Principle:
Get Things Done by using of 3 *Levels of Goals: Good, Excellent and Amazing!*

Power Questions:
What would be a Good thing for you to do each workday? How can you expand that to the Excellent Level? What would bring you to the Amazing! Level?*

***Special Note:**
I've learned that to get to the Amazing! level often involves teaming up with other people. It can be as simple as asking a family member to take out the garbage while you write 100 words of your book.

Here's my focus point: **Amazing happens with Alliances.**

Answers to Specific Time Management Questions (and Topics):

1) How do You Free Yourself from Feeling Overwhelmed—and Control Your Email Inbox?

What is a big part of feeling overwhelmed? It's the perception of everything happening at the same time. Some years ago, Richard Carlson, author of *Don't Sweat the Small Stuff*, told me, "I learned this from another speaker. He said, 'If you think of having to be in 11 cities in 10 days, then you feel overwhelmed. Instead, think of *only doing one thing at a time. You can only be in one city at a time. It's just one thing followed by another."*

There is a solution. Do **not** look at your email as the first thing you do in the morning—before you even get out of bed!

Instead, have a *Morning Ritual that empowers you*. My process takes just 4 minutes (3 minutes for meditation and 1 minute for tapping—a process of energizing me and reciting empowering affirmations).

About Controlling Your Email Inbox

a) *Use automation.* I use gmail, and my emails are automatically sorted with promotions tossed into their own folder. I can ignore them and focus on client-related emails.

b) *Set up your own rules.* You could limit yourself to viewing email at 8 AM, 12 noon, and 4:30 pm. At least, you could make a rule that you do *not* look at email one hour before going to sleep each night. You could use that hour to "cool down."

c) *Consciously cut down on the email that you get.* I've told friends that "email is for work" with me. I requested that friends keep me off their "sharing humor" list.

2) How Do You Clear Your Time for What's Most Important to You?

We return to the method of *Top Six Targets.* Just before you go to sleep at night, you identify what is most important for your next day. You will devote appropriate energy and time because you have plucked out the Most Important Tasks from the "pile" of a standard To-Do List. Also use the *Three Types of Goals (Golden Pull, Dark Boot, Green)* to help you prioritize your efforts.

3) Do High Priority Tasks; Get the Credit You Deserve — and More Clients!

What is a high priority task? Create *Effective, Brief Ways you communicate* the value you offer to prospective clients. In the previous section labeled "Work It," I emphasized that it vital to design your communication with the focus points of Story, Brief and Compelling. Another part of this is to test how you communicate. At a conference, I talked with over

72 people. In handing out my business card, I noticed that the phrase "Soar with Confidence" did *not* get the response I was looking for. I later replaced that phrase with "You can express Extreme Confidence." That opened the door for me to describe the vital distinctions of Extreme Confidence.

About Get the Credit You Deserve — and More clients

Be sure to line up your stories of how you have achieved great results for your clients. Testimonials and brief stories give a prospective client an experience. That's when their interest and emotions are engaged. That's a great start to gaining more clients.

4) Add One Hour of High Productivity Time Every Day

With *Top Six Targets*, you go straight into action on the most important tasks. This saves time. *Planning can cut wasted time and action.* For example, you can save time in terms of how you do your banking. You can do online banking or you can identify the non-crowded times to go into the bank. With *Preset the Trigger Sequence*, you do NOT procrastinate. You have set a positive Trigger, and you automatically go into action. For example, I'll often simply bring up a file and start writing. That's automatic with me. I will not hem and haw. I won't stop and get stuck in watching cat videos on YouTube. I'll just start typing. If I hit a point that I don't know what the right word is I type "___MORE___." I know that I come back to the file, and fix the difficulties later. My father is the opposite. Each sentence must be perfect before he writes the next sentence. One of my friends said, "Tom, that's why you've written 43 books, and he's written none." My point is that using both Top Six Targets and Preset the Trigger Sequence empowers you to get more done on a daily basis.

5) Increase Your Confidence as You Lead Your Own Day

Real Confidence arises from evidence. You accomplish your *Top Six Targets*, and you start believing that you are effective. You get things done. More than that, you get the *most important* things done. Good work.

6) Conquer Procrastination and Distractions

You can conquer procrastination by using the method *Preset the Trigger Sequence*. For example, I'll get going on a tough project by saying aloud, "Just get started." That is a Trigger for me to get something—anything—done so that the whole project does *not* remain a tall mountain. I get going and start cutting the project down. I keep a *Progress Log*. That gives me the momentum to get things done. For example, as of this moment, I sat down on 54 occasions, on consecutive days, to write this book. I'm 28,531 words into this project. I have *Preset the Trigger Sequence,* and I've made great progress.

How can you apply the process of Preset the Trigger Sequence to your own work?

To Conquer Distractions, Set Up "Rules"

You set up "Rules." Use a timer. Guide yourself to focus on something vital for 10 minutes, 15 minutes or more.

One of my phrases is "Amazing happens with Alliances." You can conquer procrastination when you avoid "doing something alone." Delegate, get a coach, start a project with a friend helping for 10 minutes. When I'm testing new material, I call friends and have a brief conversation and try things out. I learn from their responses and from my own experience of how things sound and feel to me.

7) Say NO and still Protect Relationships

Saying NO is often the best way to protect your time and sanity—even your health. All of us will do well to learn how to say NO and still protect relationships.

Here's an example of how one says NO effectively.

I get invited to be part of a lot of things. Sometimes, I say:

"I know your organization does great work. I appreciate your asking me to be part of this. I'm sad that I have to say NO at this time. My plate is full. How about I brainstorm with you now and see if we can find someone who can be a match for your event."

In my response, you see that I do the following:

a) Praise the person and their group.
b) Express your sadness or regret.
c) Say NO.
d) Avoid providing a reason beyond "my plate is full."
e) Find a way to help in the moment (if possible).

The sooner you say NO becomes the sooner the other person can recover and get their needs met in some other way.

Stringing people along actually drains *your* energy in that you must keep thinking about the event you don't want to attend.

When you say NO, you're saying YES to keeping yourself strong.

I often make decisions by assessing: "Does this strengthen me?"

To take good care of yourself, say NO when appropriate.

Connected to this, I've written: "You can say YES to yourself and create a foundation to be kind and strong for others." (In a Tweet, I included: #staystrong #onpurpose.)

Before you go into a situation when it's best for you to say

NO, be sure to rehearse aloud with someone you trust.

Special Section:
The *9-Minute Miracle* to Unleash the Amazing You

This section is based on material that we covered earlier in this book.

Here are the 9 minutes of actions that can empower your life.

3 minutes – Sound/Image Focused Meditation
1 minute – Tapping
2 minutes – Top Six Targets
2 minutes – Daily Journal of Victories and Blessings
1 minute – Optimize Goals: Good—Excellent—Amazing!

- **Have a Morning Ritual to Empower Your Day**

When you implement the Morning Ritual that fits you, you'll let go of dreading the morning. Each morning, I do a form of meditation that is based on some research. It's suggested that when one concentrates on one image and one sound simultaneously, then the brain can shift to "neutral."

When you have a Morning Ritual that works for you, you're making sure to avoid looking at email as your entrance into the day. For many of us, seeing email is like the house is on fire—first thing!

Instead, consider 3 minutes of meditation and then add tapping. Dr. Brenda Wade taught me this process. You tap your chest and say aloud quickly:

"I am one hundred percent loveable.

I am one hundred percent worthy.

I am one hundred percent free to be me.

I am one hundred percent safe."

Some authors suggest that tapping your chest is good for stimulating your heart chakra. You don't have to believe that. Still, these affirmations said aloud can positively impact your subconscious mind.

- **Have a Just-Before-Sleep Ritual to "Go to Sleep Happy"**

Take 2 minutes and write down your Top Six Targets for your next day. Take 2 more minutes and note the Victories and Blessings of your day in your *Daily Journal of Victories and Blessings*.

- **Take a Moment to Reconnect with "Good—Excellent—Amazing!"**

At different times in the day, you can glance at your list of goals centered about the *3 Levels of Goals: Good—Excellent-Amazing!"*

Special Section:
Get It Done ...

Pitch with Extreme Confidence

Recently, I accepted an invitation and gave a workshop *Pitch with Extreme Confidence* to an audience of Stanford Entrepreneurs and Silicon Valley Founders. The announcement for the workshop included:

> **What does it take to Pitch with Extreme Confidence?**
> This workshop gives you both the new skills and opportunities to practice them. Extreme Confidence does NOT merely come from knowledge of your text or focus area. People who pitch are often afraid because they do not know how to handle their mind going blank or an investor's toughest question. They're afraid of being embarrassed. Have you ever given a pitch and merely hoped that you would get through it without messing up? Just imagine having the Extreme Confidence to know that you can handle something — anything — going wrong.

It's about learning what seizes attention and how to handle tough questions that build a real connection with the investors. It may seem that you're talking to a group. But you're talking to individual investors. They watch for how your body language and vocal tonality show that you're on edge. Confidence is contagious. You express confidence, and the investors are confident in you—and you gain your funding. It's all about creating trust. Focus on how you say the words and how you move your body.

Here's what you'll learn:
- Experience Real Confidence
- Seize the Investors' Attention
- Answer Tough Questions with Poise
- Let Go of Fear and Nervousness
- Use Confident Body Language
- Handle Tough Moments (even if your mind goes blank)

I'm now including highlights and selected details from my workshop, *Pitch with Extreme Confidence: The Pitch Hacking Method.*

"I'm giving a speech at Sun Microsystems. It's going well. I'm feeling good. They're nodding; they're with me. Twenty minutes into the speech, my assistant, at the back of the room, waves her arms frantically, trying to get my attention.

Then she gestures: Zip up your fly! Zip up your fly!"

[Audience members laugh.]

Inside I feel like this: AHHGH! Credibility gone.

Fortunately, we're here to talk about Pitching with Extreme Confidence. Because I'm going to share methods that you'll practice during this workshop. You'll be working in Teams of Three.

We're talking about **Extreme Confidence**."

The above is the beginning of my workshop.

Extreme Confidence includes the following:
1) A level of confidence above knowing your text (of a speech, pitch or sales presentation).
2) You KNOW that you know how to adapt to anything.
3) You have skillful control over the space between you and the audience.

"Space" refers to physical space and the emotional space or connection with your audience.

Have you endured times when you hoped to just get through the text of your pitch without messing up?

What do you do if your mind goes blank?

Are you ready for that tough situation?

You want to learn how to use your body language and your vocal tonality so you come across with Extreme Confidence. Why? Because **Confidence is Contagious. You express confidence. The investors pick up that confidence. That builds trust. And trust gets funding.**

[In my workshops, I have the attendees gather in Teams of Three. In each team, one person stands up and practices the exercises. The other two people serve as a mini-audience. Then, each person gets a turn to practice the exercise.]

To practice methods of Extreme Confidence, we'll focus on the word A.I.M.

A – align body language with confidence
I – intensify Recovery Methods
M – move to narrative and humor

1. Align Body Language for Confidence
The essence of good body language:
1) Do not back away from the audience. (Stepping backwards creates emotional distance.)
2) Walk toward someone who asks you a question (one or two steps).
3) "Invite them in." (We can do that with hand gestures and asking question to engage the audience.)

We're going to have you learn to move your body in a confident way.

Now, I'll share information that has been reported by people who have worked in the FBI. They look in three places to see if you're telling the truth: face, hands and feet.

For example, I say that I have a great product and it will ultimately serve millions of people—and I'm wringing my hands.

What do you believe? My words or my wringing hands?

Subconsciously, people pick up the nervousness conveyed by the wringing hands.

To modify an old phrase: Your body speaks so loudly, I can't hear what you're saying."

Meaning that: if it's not congruent, your body language will override your words.

So, this being the case, we need to get our body language together.

We talk about the face, hands, and feet. Guess where the FBI looks first? At your feet.

So, here's what happens. Someone hits you with a *Big and*

Bad Question—something that you really hoped no investor would ask. Or you're hit with question that you didn't think about before you were standing there pitching to the investors.

Investors like to test us. They like to push us.

I've raised money for various projects, and if you can't adapt in the moment, you can't have Extreme Confidence. And you need it—because your confidence leads to trust. *And trust leads to funding.*

I had to learn—and I conditioned myself—to align my body so my heart faces the questioner's heart. I call this: *Heart Faces Heart.*

When I get a tough question, I learned to get my body to align. Why? Because we want to get those feet pointed in the right direction.

A number of people fail to get their feet pointed toward the other person. Have you ever seen someone who wants to get away from another person—while they're talking at a networking event? They're saying, "Uh-huh. I'm talking with you."

But their feet are pointed *away*. The feet are saying, 'I want to RUN!'"

What's happening here is: The feet will tell the truth.

That's why you do *Heart Faces Heart* and automatically the feet will point in the right direction.

My background with a degree in psychology—and training as an actor, feature film director and screenwriter—have all helped me excel with improvisation. **I also know how we communicate with the body. That's my training.**

We're talking about having you get used to pointing your feet in the appropriate direction—and making people feel like you're connecting with them.

The Big Idea Here is: You may think you're talking to an audience—a group—but you're actually talking to individuals. When somebody asks you a bad question, at least they're interested. They're doing you a favor. They're kind of saying: "Look, if you can handle this, I might continue to believe in you."

[At this point in the workshop I have people in Teams of Three practice responding to a "Bad Question."

Person A says, "Bad Question!"

*And the speaker (Person B) **turns and faces** Person A.*

That's practicing Heart Faces Heart.*]*

2. Intensify Recovery Methods.

Extreme Confidence is *not* just about memorizing text.

It's about being ready to recover when something goes wrong.

We're talking about *Intensify Recovery Methods*. How do you recover? You recover by being ready. By rehearsing the ways you recover.

One way to recover is to have **2 Answers for every one of 10 Worst Questions You Don't Want to Answer.**

So, with 2 Answers for each of 10 Questions, how many answers do you have? Twenty! Therefore, you're more prepared than many people aiming to give a pitch.

If you watch the TV Show *Shark Tank*, you see the investors attack with their questions. Why? They want to see if you can you stand the heat.

Recovery Method: "I'm glad you brought that up"

Someone asks you a bad question. You turn toward the person. *Heart Faces Heart.* You take one or two steps toward that person. You say, "I'm glad you brought that up."

Now, I'll give you some alternatives to "I'm glad you brought that up."

- "Amanda, I can see that's important to you."
- "I can see—your name is George? ... George, I can see that's important to you."
- "Hmmm. I haven't look at it quite that way before. I need to pause for a moment. I want my answer to be valuable to you."

I've been a professional speaker for over 16 years and a member of the National Speakers Association for over 15 years. If some kind of problem could happen on stage, I've probably walked right into it. And I've lived to tell the tale.

Here's my point. The important thing to do is **Maintain Your Poise.**

It's poise for when things are tough.

Let's go back to the tough situation I mentioned earlier. I've been giving a speech at Sun Microsystems—with the zipper down of my pants for 20 minutes.

I get the information from my assistant that my zipper has been down all this time.

I feel my stomach clutch in embarrassment and fear.

What do I do?

I nod in my assistant's direction so she can stop frantically waving her arms.

Then I turn to the audience and say, "I've just received some important information. I'll be right back."

I step off stage, go out the back door, close that door and—I zip up my pants.

Soon, I get back on stage and say, "Those of you who know what just happened ... okay."

I pause. "Those of you who don't know what just happened ... *good!*"

Hugh laughter rises from the audience. One of the longest laughs I've inspired in my speaking journey.

I thought I had lost all credibility. Still, the audience appreciated my recovery. They joined me at the autograph table and bought products.

Why? **It's about poise.** It's *not* about never making a mistake. It's about handling the mistake or the situation ... adapting with poise.

So how do we use poise connected to our Recovery Methods?

What we need is for you to "Catch the Question."

That's what we've been doing with "I'm glad you brought that up."

Or the alternatives: "George, I can see that's important to you.

Or the other response: "Hmmm. I haven't looked at it quite that way before. I'll need to pause for a moment. I want my response to be valuable to you."

When you say one of these memorized phrases, your mind is moving at 700 words a minute. While that's happening, you can figure out what to say next.

Now, let's talk about what you can do if your mind goes blank.

You don't know where you are in your pitch. You don't know what you just said, and you don't know what you need to say next.

This is something I practice with my clients. I say, "Your mind has just gone blank. Use a Recovery Method."

The Recovery Method for One's Mind Going Blank

You say, "At this moment, I want to emphasize ..."

You can be anywhere in a pitch, and you can say, "At this moment, I want to emphasize ... (and you fill in the blank)."

Here's an example: "At this moment, I want to emphasize

the big benefit my product brings to the clients is ...."

OR

"At this moment, I want to emphasize: The number one thing this product does is ...."

Then you take a pause after you say that. By the time you've used this method, your brain will go "Oh. That's right, we're supposed to be talking about _____."

Standard Way to Recover:
- Take a drink of water. If you get stuck, you can raise your hand to indicate "Just a moment." Then point to your throat as if it's dry. Have a drink of water. That will buy you some time.

I'll now give you a BONUS METHOD. If you have a concern that you might forget one of your three main points – you can write the 3 points on a Post-It Note. Then hold the little Post-It note with your thumb and forefinger. You can hide the Post-It note with your other three fingers.

This is a technique adapted from what magicians do.

You see, magicians would do certain things with their thumbs. But they would hide their thumb from you. Years ago, I did a little stage magic so I'm speaking from a bit of experience here.

I suggest a Post-It Note in your hand, *avoid* writing on your hand. Because you might perspire and… it's all blurry.

3. Move to Narrative and Humor

Humor is a special situation. It's really context sensitive.

In a recent workshop, I said, "Humor always has a target. The safest target is …"

I gestured my hand toward my chest, and Bert, an audience member, did the same and said, "Me."

I said, "Bert, just said 'me.' So everybody, Bert is the safe target!"

The audience bursts into laughter.

Narrative relates to story.

Some people are really good at "narrative" so their message is compelling. Some politicians are good at narrative—even if that narrative is not accurate—but people buy it. People feel compelled. People connect. Some politicians get re-elected based on a narrative.

We notice that some people feel safer as they communicate the data. I've worked with a number of people in Silicon Valley, California. Some people appear to feel safer as they give you the core dump.

You might ask them, "Are you going to make it to the party?"

They reply, "Well, you know, if Sarah completes the XY Table and hands off to Richard who can shape page 27 and then Amanda needs to—And if it's June and it's a Thursday. Then yes, I'll be at the party."

Instead, let's develop a compelling story.

At this moment, millions of kids are saying, "Tell me story." So, stories are in our conditioning.

Cognitive scientists, including George Lakoff, have done research on this. **There are four elements of the Narrative frame: hero, villain, victim, hero's assistant.**

Who's the hero? You are! Why? Because you are bringing something new to the marketplace. You will save the victim—that's someone who is being hurt.

The villain is whoever has created some trouble.

You have the correct solution, and you are the hero. You can place the investor as a hero with you. Or you can place the investor as the hero's assistant.

How do you make this narrative work?

I'm going to share with you a structure. You first identify the answer to this question: *Who's getting hurt?*

This is what I do as an Executive Coach and Pitch Coach: I help my client identify the right question.

You can use these questions:
- Who's getting hurt?
- Who is going to save the XY people from _____?

You may *not* actually use a question to open your pitch. Still, it's valuable—as your homework—to work with this structure.

Who is going to save these people? They're the "victim."

You can continue with: "When you join with me and invest in my project, *we* are going to save these people from the *"big problem."*"

So, we're talking about converting your text into a *story*. Because that's powerful.

A story does *not* have to be a lot of words.

You can make a story in one sentence.

One of my clients, CEO Brad Carlson said, "Tom Marcoux coached me to get more done in 10 days than other coaches in 2 years."

When I heard that, I said, "I'll hold onto that forever." Whoosh! It's on my website.

Here's the point: It's a whole story in one sentence.

As the Spoken Word Strategist, I help clients pull these sentences together—and trim out the excess.

Think of the users of your product. Think of the problem you're solving.

Use the structure. Focus on: "Who's going to save the XY

people—that's your target market—from the *big terrible problem.*"

A BONUS IDEA "Six Powerful Words":
At one point, I had a new client, Cheryl, who said, "I'm afraid."

"I'm listening. Afraid of what?" I asked, gently.

"I'm afraid that this year is *not* going to get better than last year. I'm afraid that I'm going to stay stuck. I'm afraid that I'm not going to be able to take my pitch to a higher level and actually get that funding."

"It's good to know what's actually bothering you," I began. "I *can* help you with this. Here are **Six Words** that will bring your game up—so you will have a better year—this year."

The First Three Words
The first Three Words are: **"Do Different Things."** Some people say, "What? It's that simple?"

Simple does *not* mean easy. To do different things, you need mentors, you need a coach, you need to study, and you need to rehearse in different ways.

I talked with one of my mentors. I said, "I like to take massive action."

My mentor said, "Massive PROPER action."

I agree. That would be the better way to go.

The Second Set of Three Words
Here are the other three words I shared with Cheryl: ***Think Different Thoughts.***

The only way you're going to think different thoughts is to make your thinking patterns into an "Open System."

Maybe you know some elderly people. There may be a

correlation between the more closed-off they are, and the more bitter some elderly individuals are. I know a couple of extended family members who are bitter because *nothing new can get in.*

So, I've shared the Six Words so you have a better year from this moment forward.

"Do Different Things; Think Different Thoughts."

To *Pitch with Extreme Confidence* means you KNOW, deep in your gut and in your heart, that you can adapt to anything. Therefore, you'll be able to impress the investors: *Here is somebody who is on their toes, who's good at thinking on their feet and whom I can trust.*

And trust gets funding.

Principle:
Rehearse Recovery Methods so you can adapt to anything (as part of *Extreme Confidence*).

Power Questions:
Of the Recovery Methods, what grabs your attention? What Recovery Methods will you rehearse today?

Book 2
Get Stronger

Imagine that you feel strong. Right now. In this moment. What would you do? How could you make your life better?

When I speak on the topic of *"Break Free and Get It Done,"* I include insights about how we can get stronger. Some people suggest that people become physically weaker with age. Actually, I've met people who embarked on a physical training regimen and became stronger in their 50s than they were in their 20s. Amazing! And doable.

More than that, we can become stronger because we can protect our energy by doing wise actions.

This section of the book will support you to take action so you can quiet down the feelings of "overwhelmed."

Get stronger and develop significant personal energy. Then, you can do those tough things that will raise your life to higher levels of success and happiness.

Increase Your Strength – Method #1

The Secret to Help You Decide and Bring in Real Success

"I know I should do this," Mark said. "But I don't think I can afford it."

The day before I had an in-depth conversation with Mark about where his business was—but more importantly, about what great things will happen when he fulfills his *own potential* and fulfills the potential of his business. Still, Mark was stuck.

As an Executive Coach, I've helped people do amazing things. What is required for that? Breaking out of your limitations involves making a shift to an *Empowered Mindset.*

Here are three *Vital Elements of Making the Life-Changing Decision.* We'll use the W.I.N. process:

1. Wonder about "the Signs"

Pay attention. Are you saying, "I know I should do this"? Your own subconscious mind is telling you something important. You may also see things in your environment. Your brain has the Reticular Activating System (RAS). The RAS becomes sensitive to the environment. If you're thinking about buying a specific brand of car, you start seeing those cars everywhere.

Perhaps, you start seeing memes on social media about people who took the right risk and made their lives full of abundance, creativity and adventure. That's the Universe saying, "You can have wonderful things in your life, too. Step forward in faith."

Get clear on this distinction:

The Voice of Fear says: *"Contract, hide, do not take an appropriate risk."*

The Voice of Intuition says: *"Expand, experiment, take an appropriate risk."*

Make space to hear your intuition.

2. Identify if you're scared AND excited

Growing to a Higher Level calls on you to stretch. It is natural for you to feel some fear. In fact, in the right situation, it is required. Required? Yes. You are kicking off the mud of your Previous Chapter of Life. You're going to need to perform on a level that you've never experienced before.

If you feel scared, I'm with you. Just before I directed my first feature film, I was scared, deep in my bones. What did I do? I personally drew 801 storyboard images. I made sure that I knew the story up-down-sideways and through and through. Total preparation.

Here's something else: my co-producer said, "Tom, you play a leading role—as one of the characters." What?! My stress would already be off the charts. But I knew: Things were in place. I had the team, the script, filming equipment and a tiny budget. Our budget was too low to gain the actor we wanted. I could try to "play it safe" and wait. Or I could do what my gut and heart said: "Direct this film now. Play that character. Do NOT let this chance get away!"

I'm so glad that I took the risk. It literally changed my life! I went into different circles and met the love of my life. I even became an educator, training MBA students at Stanford University. Because I took the right risk.

What has you both scared AND excited? Is this your Big Chance? Find out.

Here's my phrase: *To stand out, find out what you stand for.*

My friend, I invite you to *Stand Up for Your New and Great Chapter of Your Own Life!*

3. Nurture and Expand Your Capabilities

Will taking this risk Increase Your Capabilities? That's the question to consider. Many of us notice that (often) we don't regret what we did. We regret what we did NOT do. Some time ago, I had little money. Still, I invested in getting coaching and taking workshops and online courses. Why? It was all about Increasing My Capabilities.

My friend: Increasing Your Capabilities is just like having gold that massively increases in value. That's right. When you expand your skills and personal experience, you have some "gold" that truly appreciates in value. You cannot go wrong.

Let's say you have the choice between getting a huge-screen TV or putting the money into some coaching. Make the decision to Increase Your Capabilities. Why? You'll be able to afford multiple TVs (if the courses you take and the coaching you get are about improving your prowess in business).

Special Note: Will the decision increase your capabilities and upgrade your circle of contacts? Recently, I attended a conference and made so many high-value connections—it was a true joy and opportunity.

Let's remember these *Vital Elements to Make the Best Decisions to Unleash Financial Abundance in Your Life:*

W – Wonder about "the Signs"

I – Identify if you're scared AND excited

N – Nurture and expand Your Capabilities

Make better decisions.

Take an appropriate risk.

Become proud yourself.

Principle:
Invest in yourself and expand your capabilities.

Power Questions:
What could you do to expand your capabilities and "raise the game you're playing"? (That is, how can you gain skills and join a higher level in your industry?)

Increase Your Strength – Method #2

Focus on a Positive Idea and Step Forward

Here is a guest article by one of my mentors.

Guest article:

When Times are Tough, Someone with an Idea is Needed
by Dottie Walters

My father left when I was 13. To support my Mom, I worked at a midnight bakery. Then I discovered an unlimited secret treasure—the public library. I learned from the greatest minds who ever lived: Ralph Waldo Emerson, Catherine the Great, Tom Edison, Will Shakespeare, Amelia Earhart, George Washington Carver, Benjamin Franklin, and more.

What amazed me was that every great person had faced disasters and disappointment. Jack Dempsey, the champion boxer, told me., "Champions are the ones who get up when they can't." Bill Marriott of the Marriott hotels, wrote, "Failure? I never encountered it! I have met only temporary setbacks."

My high school English teacher pulled me out of my regular class for journalism. After I scrubbed the floors, I wrote articles and a shoppers column, late at night when there were no customers. My journalism teacher said she had never received homework on slightly soiled bakery bags before!

Later, my husband, our two little children, and I moved into a small home, but the recession hit. We could not make the house payments. There were no jobs. A free copy of the local newspaper, was thrown at my door. Then I saw it in my imagination!—with the same Shoppers Column I had written for my high school newspaper!

But I had no typewriter. I ran next door and borrowed my neighbor's typewriter. However, my rickety old baby stroller was designed for one child. I thought a moment, and grabbed our bed pillows—tied them on the back of the stroller with clothesline rope creating a second seat. The wheel came off the stroller, and I took off my shoe and hit the wheel back on.

When I got to the newspaper office, I saw the sign: "NO HELP WANTED!" The warm kind voice of my friend newspaper man Benjamin Franklin spoke to me: "Observe Dottie, dear!" he said. "If they do not need help it is because they have no advertisers. Go in and offer to buy advertising space at wholesale. Sell it to the local merchants at retail in the form of your delightful shoppers column. I promise you, the difference in a month's time, will make your mortgage payment. Remember, you are a housewife—a customer. Tell them you will write the column from the customer's standpoint!"

I brought out my sample column and my high school "press pass" and asked that the publisher to sell me advertising space at wholesale. I proposed to write a weekly shoppers column "Window Wishing." That dear editor answered, "Yes."

When my shoes wore out, I cut cardboard and put pieces into them. Lots of people said "no" to my sales talk. My friends from the library had taught me to take action. I determined that my family would not lose their home, and I figured out what I could do right then.

Later, I noticed stories about service club meetings: Kiwanis, Rotary, Lions Club, Chamber of Commerce. They named the officers: the owners of businesses I had been trying to sell. I would be a speaker at those meetings—and bring a basket to pick up their business cards and hold a drawing for a prize. I would tell them about my shoppers column and what we housewives wanted in customer service. Then I could sell my ads to members over the phone! But I had no car or babysitter. I remembered my friend wo loaned me the typewriter. Then, I took care of her children so she could go bowling with her husband, in return for the loan of her old car, and the care of my children at noon when I spoke at the service club luncheons.

By this means, within 18 months, I built my advertising business to all of Southern California. I opened 4 offices, and employed 285 people. We soon had over 4,000 continuing contract advertising accounts. I build that business by speaking free to service clubs. One day a man said after my talk, "What would you change to speak for my employees?" His check was the beginning of my speaking career on four continents, the writing of my books, the publishing of my magazine about speaking, and the opening of our international speakers' bureau.

The achievers of the world call out to us with great enthusiasm: "Follow Me! You are needed!" Listen to them. When times are tough, all that is needed is someone with a great idea. That someone is you.

– Dottie Walters

* * *

I appreciate Dottie's point: "When times are tough, all that is needed is someone with a great idea."

How do we get great ideas?

"If you don't have time to read, you don't have the time (or the tools) to write. Simple as that." – Stephen King

Reading, listening to audiobooks, watching TED talks are ways to get started. Want great ideas?—be around great ideas!

Principle:
Make yourself "fertile ground" for great ideas.

Power Question:
How will you get yourself around great ideas? (Reading, listening to audiobooks, watching TED talks and more)

Increase Your Strength — Method #3

Step into Your New Chapter of Life

"The past can be understood as Part I of our story. ...What I really hunger to do now is to tell a new story about my life, one that is full of possibility, transcends limitation and says something different about who I REALLY AM." – Liz Stolz Kughn

Over the years when I reflected on reading the above material from Liz Stolz Kughn, I thought of this phrase: **"That was Chapter One of my life; I'm living in Chapter Two."**

Have you noticed that some people are stuck in the past? On other hand, others are overcoming the past. These people spread their wings and take to the sky.

One of my favorite quotes is:

"In truth, I am a verb." – Steve Chandler

When you are a verb, you are *not* stuck. You don't fruitlessly pine for the past. You are present-focused. If you've lost something important, you still cherish what is good in this present moment.

I taught college level Comparative Religion for 14 years. Then, things changed and that chapter of my life ended. I grieved. Still, I had a positive approach, and I said, "I wonder what good is happening in my New Chapter of Life."

My friend, are you in a tough transition at this time?

Declare that this is a New Chapter of Your Life.

Identify what you want this chapter of your life to be about. We can hit targets when we have identified such targets. (Return to an earlier section of this book about *3 Levels of Goals: Good—Excellent—Amazing*).

Principle:

Declare a New Chapter of Life.

Power Questions:

What do you *want* this chapter of your life to be about? What do you want to bring into your life? What do you want to drop from your life? … What are you grateful for at this moment of your life?

Increase Your Strength – Method #4

Get in Motion – "Motion Brings Clarity"

Harry, a new client, said, "Before I do that, I want to feel certain. I want some clarity."

In an extended conversation, I shared with Harry: "I hear you. You want certainty and clarity. I have something to share with you. I've seen in my own life and with a number of clients this truth: **Motion Brings Clarity."**

Harry's faced scrunched up. He wasn't quite with this idea yet.

"Picture this," I began. "You and I stand in a valley. We've been told that there are some mountain peaks that will take our breath away. We can't see much in this valley. So, we start walking upwards. At a certain point, we can see some other peaks—of other mountains. You tell me, 'Hey, look to the right. See that? I want to go over there.'"

Harry smiled.

"So, my point is…?" I asked.

"I couldn't see *that* mountain peak from deep in the

valley," Harry said.

"Exactly. *Motion Brings Clarity.*"

Guest Article:

Have Faith in Your Journey
by Libba Cooperman

I was raised in the Jewish faith, but I was not touched in my heart by that particular faith. Then, my religion was the hippie faith. I was on the streets, partying, drinking and engaging in other self-destructive behavior. I was trying to fill up holes of a dysfunctional family life. By the time I reached 29 years of age, I was like a desert, barren and desolate, with nothing to live for and no plans for the future.

Then, my sister came to live with me. She was by herself with four children to raise. She was praying constantly, and her Bahá'í prayers just permeated the walls of my apartment. She was about to have a baby, and I started to attend midwife classes with her. When my niece was born, it felt like I was being reborn at the same time. I was like a cup that had been filled with garbage. And when you're full, nothing can come in. I was being emptied of my old lifestyle so I began to ask my sister about the Bahá'í faith.

The one thing that attracted me the most to the Bahá'í faith was the idea that there is a golden thread that runs through the religions—in that God gives guidance in every age with masters like Buddha, Christ, Mohammed, and more. My sister had been trying to tell me about her faith for about fifteen years. But until I learned who Christ was, and had a personal relationship with Him, how could I understand the rest of the prophesies?

With the Bahá'í faith, I came to realize that God's eternal

plan for humankind is one of "progressive revelation."

I took the spiritual principle of unity and the oneness of humankind, and it led me to seek out avenues of interest like joining the National Association for the Advancement of Colored Peoples (NAACP)—an unusual move for a white, Southern woman.

When I moved to California, I wanted to continue having diversity in my life. I joined the local NAACP chapter so I could have some deep lasting friendships with some African Americans, especially because I had dear friends when I grew up in the South. I had attended an integrated high school.

My role is to say, "I support you." I do whatever is needed, like work in the kitchen or sell tickets to fundraising events.

It's been a journey of several years, but as I kept searching, I found a higher purpose for my life and that my job on this planet is to love and to serve.

– Libba Cooperman

* * *

I appreciate how Libba shared her journey. She said, "I took the spiritual principle of unity and the oneness of humankind, and it led me to seek out avenues of interest like joining the National Association for the Advancement of Colored Peoples (NAACP)—an unusual move for a white, Southern woman."

I note that she kept in motion and found her path.

Principle:
Motion Brings Clarity.

Power Questions:

How are you going to get in motion? What can you do that's new and different? How will you reward yourself for doing new actions?

Increase Your Strength – Method #5

Bring Peace and Empowerment to Your Daily Life

To feel stronger, you need two types of energy: a) calm-in-the-storm energy and b) get-things-done energy.

Some of us find that we feel inner peace when we connect with the idea that human beings are spiritually connected.

Guest Article:

Deity is Water
By Johanna E. Mac Leod

Have you caught a bit of broadcast news and heard about someone's cruelty to another person—and it bothered you?

Or maybe you've wondered about how some extremists use religion as a justification for terrible acts.

Recently, just as I was drifting off to sleep, an idea blazed across the expanse of my mind.

Picture this. **Deity is water. Each human being is a vessel.**

Imagine that Deity's essence is a large infinite ball of water.

Let's say you're a bowl, and you grow up among bowls. All you know are bowls. In fact, you might say that bowl people have a "bowl God" because they see themselves in what they picture to be Divine.

On the other side of the ocean are goblets. And they only know themselves as goblets. So, they have a "goblet God."

But Deity fills ALL bowls and ALL goblets. Deity is ONE. Deity is in everyone.

Water will take the shape of any vessel it fills. The vessels may differ dramatically, but what fills them is the same.

Our problem—that is human beings' problem—is that we see ourselves as vessels—as bowls or goblets.

Do we humans get caught up in looking at vessels? Sure we do. Research reveals that tall people and "pretty" people get treated better than others. They get the jobs and the promotions.

Imagine that we approach each other with compassion. Then, we might make more space for individuals' perceptions.

Let's try the perspective: *Deity is water. Each human being is a vessel.*

Many blessings on your journey.

—Johanna E. Mac Leod

* * *

I appreciate Johanna's point about *"Deity is water. Each human being is a vessel."*

This reminds me to move beyond the surface appearance.

A number of spiritual paths emphasize that human beings share a true connection.

"The most authentic thing about us is our capacity to create, to overcome, to endure, to transform, to love and to be greater than our suffering." – Ben Okri

Recently, I heard two friends say these comments: "I hate people who drive like that!" and "I hate those people. They don't care if people die. Those people just care about money."

I pause when hearing people toss around the word "hate." It's understandable that people get angry about the *actions* of other people. Still, to default to the word "hate" can cause real problems.

"It is above all by the imagination that we achieve perception and compassion and hope." – Ursula K. Le Guin

Can you and I imagine that other people, for the most part, are trying to cope?

"Be kind, for everyone you meet is fighting a hard battle."
– attributed to Plato

Can we imagine that there is a bit of divinity in each person that seeks to demonstrate connection and compassion?

Principle:
Imagine that we're all connected. We are.

Power Questions:

How will you let your first judgmental thought flow by? Will you memorize certain phrases to shift your thinking? How will you be kind to yourself so you have more energy to be flexible—and patient?

Increase Your Strength – Method #6

Listen to Inner Guidance

Do you listen to inner guidance or your intuition? Do you take action based on your intuition?

Guest article:

Discover Your Life Purpose
By Linda L. Chappo

I've talked to many people about discovering their life purpose. Some people know at a very young age what they are meant to do, so they pursue that particular path. My friend, author Tom Marcoux, discovered his purpose at nine years of age. Other people, like myself, didn't discover it until midlife. Perhaps your previous occupation was a stepping stone or a training ground to something more suitable. For some women, giving birth and raising a family is their life purpose. That's their contribution to the world.

Each life is a valuable, worthy and unique contribution. Living a spiritual life means finding your particular way of serving the world, a way that only you can do. Think about what you are passionate about. What makes your heart sing? That's what God would have you do. One thing I discovered about having dreams and goals is when we go to Spirit first with our request and retain an open mind, the dream or goal is revealed and is sometimes redefined for us. We are often redirected in ways that benefit us more. Spend time in meditation. Open your mind and heart. Make it a goal to discover your life purpose.

Here's an example of my experience. When I lived in Chicago many years ago, I thought I wanted to pursue a life as a writer and artist. I wanted to make a difference in the world. Guidance counselors encouraged me to choose one goal. I chose to become a writer. My inner guidance encouraged me to do something else, which was to live my dream. I had a spiritual epiphany six months prior, during a writer's conference. So I quit college in Chicago, moved to California (where I always wanted to live) and enrolled in a college for graphic arts. I was able to achieve both goals by taking writing classes. It doesn't stop there. Those goals are merely stepping stones to something greater: for me it is a life as a spiritual teacher. And that too is a stepping stone to something much larger. That's my purpose and most everything I've done contributes in some way to that purpose.

If you're like many people, you have your limiting beliefs or thoughts of unworthiness. With Spirit guiding the way, limiting thoughts are surpassed by thoughts of new and wonderful possibilities. We've each heard the phrase, "With God all things are possible." This is true, although not always in the time frame or in the form we may imagine.

That, for me, is often the best part: the surprise of new experiences. It's understandable that we may have to work on ourselves or do some preparation for the dream or goal.

There was a time when I knew I would soon be unemployed. I wanted my next job to be different. After some exploration I came up with two prerequisites for my future career: being with lots of people and traveling. Then a friend told me about job openings with an airline company. At first I was concerned, "They won't hire me because of my age, my appearance or lack of pertinent skills, etc." I became my own judge and jury. My inner guidance encouraged me to just show up for the interview. I prepared myself with a new suit and a new attitude. At the end of the day I passed the tests and made all the cuts. I had an airline ticket to Chicago, a chance at a second interview, and a renewed enthusiasm. In the end, I wasn't hired by the company, but it was an exhilarating experience. I had faith that something better would occur. If we remain open-minded, happy surprises do occur.

– Linda L. Chappo

* * *

I appreciate Linda's point: "I had faith that something better would occur."

I would call Linda's journey with applying for a flight attendant job *an adventure*. What makes up an interesting life? It's stepping out of our comfort zone and trying new things.

Principle:
Remain open-minded, and happy surprises do occur.

Power Questions:

In what areas of your life would you welcome a happy surprise? Do you relate to a Higher Power? Do you ask for inner guidance? Do you take action based on inner guidance?

Increase Your Strength – Method #7

Use *Extreme Confidence* to Quiet Down Fear … Pitch and Gain Funding

"I think I have the text of my pitch fully memorized," my new client, Alana, said.

"And?" I asked, seeing something in her facial expression.

"I'm still nervous!" she said.

"It's understandable," I began. Then, in an extended conversation, I introduced her to my term *Extreme Confidence.*

Extreme Confidence includes two things:
1) You KNOW that you know how to adapt to anything comes up during your pitch.
2) You effectively control the "space" between you and the audience members.

When I refer to the "space" between you and audience members, I'm talking about whether you're connected or separate from the individuals in your audience.

When you develop the skills of Extreme Confidence, you quiet down fear and nervousness.

Develop the Skill to Get More Time to Think
An investor asks a really tough question while you're pitching to a group. You can say, "I need to pause for a moment. I want my response to be valuable to you." You just gave yourself some time to think. Even while you say the above sample comment, your brain is thinking at 700 words a minute. You might even come with the answer just as you finish with "…valuable to you."

Give Yourself "Room to Experiment"
Recently, I was asked about how to include a case study when one is talking to a prospective client.

I replied, "I'll brainstorm here. You might try this: 'I helped Joe upgrade his website, and he went from 10 new e-list subscribers per month to 1,237 new e-list subscribers per month. The rate of new clients he gained went from 1 per month to 4 per month — with a long-term value of each client as $6,000. So that was a net gain of …"

When I said, "I'll brainstorm here," I gave myself the room to experiment. After I said the above details, I might have come up with a better idea. Then, I could have continued with: "As I was sharing the details I just gave you, I had an another idea. This might even be better …"

The Golden Key: Rehearsing with Experimenting
There is a *Paradox of a Good Pitch:* Use a script for *Selected Phrases* and have space for improvising.

You need both.

How do you come up with the Effective Selected Phrases? You do rehearsing with experimenting.

I'll give you an example. Recently, I went to a conference that included a number of life coaches, healers and others. I experimented with ways to start a conversation. Some ways worked better than others. Then I started saying, "How do you help people?" My tone was warm, and my approach was friendly curiosity. That worked well.

I also experimented with ways to respond to the question: "What do you do?"

After a number versions, and while I watched the faces of my conversation partners, I landed on this:

"I help people fulfill big dreams. Primarily, I help business owners and executives speak so powerfully that they get a lot of YES's."

As I said the above, I gestured with my hands as if a bunch of YES's, like gifts, came toward my heart.

In terms of developing your pitch, practice in front of a number of "test audiences."

* * *

In summary, realize that rehearsing with experimenting is an important part of developing your best pitch to gain funding. Consider working with a coach so you pick the best details and *Effective Selected Phrases*.

Principle:
Rehearse *and* experiment during such sessions.

Power Questions:
When and with whom will you rehearse? Who gives you a safe "space" to experiment?

Get Credit for It:
(*Special Section:* Get people to know you via an e-book at your website.)

How do people know that you're really good?

They need some form of experience of you.

One way is to give a speech. Another way is offer a free e-book at your website. To make this clear, I'll offer a case study.

I'll now share the text of a 14-page e-book that I offer at my websites.

Develop Your Extreme Confidence and Seize Advantages in Business and Life

Yes—you can do better in life and business.

You need to be skilled to overcome *The Deadly Three: Fear, Hesitation, and Procrastination.*

How? Build your "Extreme Confidence Skills."

In this e-book, I'll share how to "Overcome Fear and

Hesitation."

More than that ... I'll share a *Golden Key for Real Success*.

The Golden Key for Real Success: Replace Willpower with a System

Researchers at Stanford University identified that willpower is like a muscle; it wears out as the day goes along. That's why I eat salad for breakfast.

To perform at your best, you need something more powerful than just being confident about "the text" – that is, the actual words of your speech, pitch or sales presentation.

Here's the solution: You learn special methods I call "Recovery Methods." Then, you're confident that you can handle anything that comes up. With this extra level of confidence, you rise to what I call *Extreme Confidence*. Then you can *Perform at Your Best*.

A prime element of Extreme Confidence is training in ways to adapt to anything that arises.

For example, let's say you're giving a speech, pitch or sales presentation... What if your mind goes blank? Extreme Confidence skills provide you with Recovery Methods so you handle tough moments with poise.

Your Benefits with This E-book:
- Learn practical methods to raise your confidence level
- Identify actual building blocks for improving your own performance

Topics:
1. Perform at Your Best
2. Overcome Fear and Procrastination
3. Use Your Personal Brand to Connect and Get People

to Buy What You're Offering

1. Perform at Your Best

What are the best results that can manifest from your performance—perhaps, a speech, pitch or sales presentation?

A number of us realize that to perform at our best, even during a vital meeting with your boss or even a tough phone call, it helps to rehearse.

Here's the important distinction: Rehearsing the text is not enough. You do better when you rehearse *Recovery Methods*.

Recovery Methods are techniques we use to regain our balance when something goes wrong. Recovery Methods are a foundational part of Extreme Confidence.

Extreme Confidence is when you KNOW that you know how to adapt to anything that arises.

For the times when you need to be on your toes, you need to be able to adapt and pivot quickly.

Here's an example. I was giving a speech at IBM. My mind went BLANK. I was stuck. Inside, I felt: "Augh! I'm so embarrassed."

What could I do? What would you do?

On the inside, I was panicking. On the outside, I took a breath and said, "I'll need to pause for a moment. My brain needs more RAM."

Those tech folks at IBM thought that a RAM (Random Access Memory) joke was hilarious!

As I work with a client, I help her find her own language—those words that feel comfortable specifically for her. Then we practice. I call out: "Your mind just went blank.

Use a Recovery Method."

This helps my client rise to the level of Extreme Confidence. She gets to the point that she KNOWS that she can recover—and truly connect with her audience.

Conventional Approach: **Rehearse the text.**
vs.
Extreme Confidence Approach: **Rehearse Recovery Methods, too.**

Here's the Point: *You rehearse Recovery Methods so you feel an extra layer of confidence throughout your presentation.*

Special Note:
Earlier I mentioned: *The Golden Key for Real Success: Replace Willpower with a System.*

When I work with a client, we plug the person's unique situation into a number of *systems.*

Here is an example.

One of my clients, Susan, wanted to give a speech. I introduced her to *Elements that Create a Great Connection with the Audience (a system).* As part of this process, I worked with Susan so she had options:

- 3 options for a bit of self-deprecating humor
- 3 options for a detail that shows your vulnerability
- 3 options for a detail that reveals your enthusiasm that got you connected with [her topic]. (I said, "We put this into a story. Your enthusiasm will wash over the audience. Enthusiasm is attractive.")

After we had the options, we could test which elements

were a good fit for Susan, and we could see how test audiences responded.

My point is: With a system, you do NOT have to force yourself to create a great performance. Working with a coach makes the whole process doable and often so powerful that you're surprised.

> "Tom Marcoux helped me unearth deeply emotional and humorous moments in my speech to move the hearts of the audience. He was there for me unconditionally. He went above and beyond anything that I expected. During every interaction that I had with Tom, I felt that I learnt something profound. I highly recommend for anyone who wants to give a great speech that you work with Tom Marcoux as your Speech Coach and Spoken Word Strategist."
> – Krishna Noru, Award-winning Speaker

1. Drop Fear and Procrastination

"I just can't get myself to get to the gym," Sam says.

"I don't know what happens. Somehow, I just don't get around to rehearsing before giving the presentation. And then I have to wing it," Anita says.

Why do we procrastinate? Researchers note much of it arises from 1) anticipation of pain and 2) not knowing what to do. Even not knowing what to do causes pain. So, we're back to pain causing procrastination.

Additionally, what does fear do to us? Many of us report that we're afraid of something going wrong and causing us pain.

I submit to you that procrastination arises from fear.

Conventional Approach: **Try to tough out fear and pain.**
vs.
Extreme Confidence Approach: **Place a system so you automatically do something positive when a Trigger hits you.**

A system can be as simple as "send a follow-up email immediately upon hanging up the phone." A system does not have to be elaborate. The point is to make your next action into something that's automatic.

Successful people I've interviewed have demonstrated that they are skilled at dealing with fear and procrastination. They move forward at an extraordinary pace. Successful people do NOT rely on "I feel like it."

Additionally, relying on willpower is the path to disaster. Why? Willpower wears out as the day goes along. Researchers note that we experience a form of fatigue arising from the exercise of our will with choice after choice.

Fortunately, I've developed a process that helps my clients and audiences. I call it S.P.A. (Many of us would like to relax at a spa. Creating success through S.P.A. leads to more "spa moments.")

S – start well
P – preset
A – act

1. Start well

My client Marina said, "It's just getting started that's hard for me." I replied, "What you need is a system. That is, we set a pattern."

She mentioned that she was having trouble "getting around to renewing her driver's license." I said, "How about you use this as your system? Put the page from the

Department of Motor Vehicles right in front of your desktop monitor. Place your passwords-book next to the DMV form. So tomorrow, it's like you have already started. Remember two ideas: 1) *Worst First*—do the tough task first and 2) Make it easy for you to get in motion. (I call this the *"Easy Part Start."*)

An important element of "start well" is to set a "starting ritual." Researchers note that many successful people have some daily habit that gets them into action fast.

One of my clients, Amanda tells herself, "Just write. Toss clay on the table." This is Amanda's way of assuring herself that she can return and revise her writing (similar to a sculpture shaping the clay into a work of art).

2. Preset

To overcome procrastination, use this method: *"Preset the Trigger Sequence."*

First, I'll identify a Trigger Sequence. Something in your environment (or even a recurring thought) pushes you into a reaction. The trigger plus your reaction is the *Trigger Sequence*.

Fortunately, you can take control. Before you step into a "hot situation," make decisions about what your positive action could be. Such a positive action would replace an automatic negative reaction.

For example, Janet returns home and feels like reaching for cookies. Fortunately, she has "preset" the situation with apples set out on the dining room table. Instead of reaching for a cookie, she grabs an apple. It works for her.

The point is: Janet knows she will be hit by the Trigger of "I'm home, and I'm hungry." However, she has already "Preset the Trigger Sequence" to help her take a healthy action.

3. Act

Sam, one of my clients, said, "I'm afraid of just acting in a haphazard way. Doing something wrong is worse than doing nothing!"

Within an extended conversation, I guided Sam with two principles:

a)   Motion Brings Clarity
b)   If in doubt, leave it out.

a)   *Motion Brings Clarity*

We'd like to avoid every misstep. However, it's like we're standing in a valley. When you start walking up the mountain, soon you'll be able to see new peaks (new choices), you could not see from the floor of the valley. Taking steps forward and upward, yields new clarity.

b)   *If in doubt, leave it out.*

Still, you can protect yourself as you take action. For example, recently I received a email confirmation notice of an appointment with the president of an organization. I could respond by simply clicking "yes" (for "yes I am attending").

However, I saw that my name was misspelled. I had the thought, "If I send an email to correct this person's misspelling, it might bother her. If would be as if I'm criticizing her and we have not even met yet."

So, I used my focus-point: "If in doubt, leave it out." I just clicked "yes" and left the idea of correcting the spelling of my name for during the in-person meeting.

In summary, to overcome procrastination (born of fear), "get strategic with it!" Use the process of S.P.A., so you can get in motion. Such action welcomes new opportunities.

2. Use Your Personal Brand to Connect and Get People to Buy What You're Offering

Your personal brand is how you become Top of Mind with the person. You're memorable.

Your personal brand is the answer to the question: "What are you best known for?" It's also a promise: "This is what you can count on me to do."

You can make your personal brand memorable through the Effective Use of Story.

Conventional Approach: **You recite an "Elevator Speech."**
vs.
Extreme Confidence Approach: **1) Use an Elevator Dialogue, and 2) Use a story and a powerful quote.**

Important Insight: An Elevator Speech often breaks rapport.

Here's a typical Elevator Speech situation.
Cheryl asks George a question:
Cheryl: "So, what do you do?"
George (shifts into Elevator Speech mode): "I'm a financial wizard who helps people like you build a Financial Fortress."

Here's the problem: George recites the "Elevator Speech," and he sounds like a commercial! Cheryl and George were having a real conversation. Then George jumps out of the conversation and sounds artificial!

Here's the Solution: The Elevator Dialogue.

Cheryl: "Wendy, what do you do?"

Wendy: "Well ... I'm curious. Have you or someone you know—a friend or family member—had an MRI exam?"

Cheryl: "My cousin Sam had an MRI. It was awful. They put in him into something like a morgue drawer. He only had 1 inch and half above his nose. Just before that, they asked him, 'Do you have claustrophobia? He now knows that he has claustrophobia! He said, 'They offered me a valium. I should have said, 'I'll take TWO.'"

Wendy: "I hear you, Cheryl. That bothers me. And that's why I'm glad about what I do. I bring Open MRI Exam machines to medical facilities. Open MRI Exam machines prevent a situation, like the one that happened to your cousin Sam."

Years ago, I used an Elevator Dialogue. I was literally on an elevator at Academy of Art University where I teach graduate students. By the end of descending two floors, this literary agent gave me his card. And I gave him my card. Believe me, as the author of 43 books, I was glad to use an Elevator Dialogue to make a great first impression!

Use a Story to Avoid Natural Resistance

With MBA students at Stanford University, I had a student hold up a hand, palm facing me. I pushed on the student's hand, and he pressed back. This illustrated a Natural Resistance.

When you express an Elevator Speech, you can cause yourself trouble by instigating Natural Resistance.

Here's the Solution: Offer an Effective Story.

An Effective Story goes under the radar and avoids inspiring Natural Resistance. When you tell a story, you do not slam the listener with an oppressive opinion. Instead, you take the person on a journey. You give him or her an experience.

Conventional Approach: Speak directly using logic to push your vision forward.
vs.
Extreme Confidence Approach: Invite them in. Use a story to avoid natural resistance.

What does it take to tell an effective story?
1) Start with "Who's getting hurt?" This is a quick way to identify the victim. Additionally, you identify the villain as the person or group that creates the problem.
2) Identify the Hero. (In a pitch situation, you could identify that investors who work with you with also be heroes.)
3) Provide suspense by showing how tough the situation is.
4) Provide the triumphant ending. The listeners get to feel great as they experience the uplifting conclusion to the story.

A story does not have to be elaborate. One can do a natural lead-in to the story. Here's an example. Jackson comes to his supervisor Mary with a problem.

"I just can't get the people in Dept. XY on board with the new initiative," Jackson says.

"I hear you. That can be really tough to endure," Mary begins. "This reminds me of how I saw a guy lead some people at the previous company I worked for. Would you like to hear what he did to turn things around?" Mary asks.

"Yes. I'll take anything now."

And, Mary launches into the story.

Let's say your personal brand is: "I provide creative solutions that save the client money."

Here's an example:

Matthew: "I provide creative solutions that save clients' money. For example, some time ago, I was a unit production manager on a feature film. We're near the end of the filming schedule. We're running out of money. Still, we haven't filmed the meeting of the two romantic leads. The script called for them to meet on a bus.

"That's expensive. You pay for renting the bus, street permits with the city, hiring off-duty police officers, feeding the extras, hiring the bus driver and more.

'I went to the Producer, Alicia, and said, 'I have access to an apartment. We could build an elevator set in the living room. The guy and gal can meet on the elevator.'

"The producer said, 'Do it.'

"The she said, 'Matthew, I can always count on you to come up with a creative solution that saves me money.'

This story is particularly effective because the point is said at the beginning, and then the point is affirmed with an actual quote from the happy producer, Alicia.

Recently, a client asked me, "How can I get people to realize the benefit I provide, so they hire me?"

I replied: "You might try this: 'I helped Joe upgrade his website and he went from 10 e-list subscribers per month to 1,237 e-list subscribers per month. The rate of new clients he gained went from 1 per month to 4 per month—with a long-term value of each client as $6,000. So that was a net gain of ...'"

In summary ...
- Extreme Confidence is when you KNOW that you

know how to adapt to anything.
- The Golden Key for Real Success: *Replace Willpower with a System*

* * * * *

Using a free e-book to introduce your expertise can be helpful for you to establish your expert-status in the mind of the website visitor.

In essence, you "get credit" for your expertise and professionalism. This is a great step on your way to helping the client choose to hire you.

Well done!

Bonus Material

In this section, *I will directly address several situations* and the effective methods for you to be at your best and accomplish your objectives.

Bonus Material #1

Use the "Power of Three" for Real Success!

"How do I know which product is going to really work in the marketplace?" my new client, Andy, asked.

"You don't," I replied. "What really helps is to use 'The Power of Three.'"

The Power of Three is a process that empowers you to try things in the marketplace, to stay strong and to maintain your focus.

We'll use the T.O.P. process:

T – take three to the marketplace
O – optimize three and no more

P – power-up "imperfect action"

1. Take three to the marketplace

When you take three products to the marketplace, you have three times the chance that you'll find something that truly resonates with your target market.

People like a choice.

As a professional speaker, I provide the event planner/meeting planner with my three top speech topics:

- Get It Done, Get Stronger, Get Credit for It – Power Time Management
- Get the Big YES: Use Extreme Confidence to Get Clients and Get It Done!*
- Pitch with Extreme Confidence: The Pitch Hacking Method

[* Get the Big YES *also serves as an online class. For information:* tomsupercoach@gmail.com]

Which one will resonate more with the meeting planner or her group? I don't know.

… not until I send the three choices as visible through my three speaker one sheets (they look like flyers).

Allow the marketplace to let you know what can turn "red hot."

2. Optimize three and no more

Focus is a crucial part of business success. It's important to avoid getting distracted. Similarly, you'll do better to avoid diluting your power, resources and attention. Pick three things and avoid trying to push too many things at once. Over the years, I've written 43 books. Still, I focus on marketing only three top speeches at this time.

Now it's your turn. What are the three best candidates (products/services) that you can promote now?

3. Power-up "imperfect action"

Waiting for the perfect time or the perfect form of your product can cause you to falter. Sometimes, perfectionists fail because they're not shipping out their product.

Years ago, one of my friends said, "Creating a cure for no known disease." He was referring to those engineers who fall in love with an idea, create a company, but later find out that no market wants what they're offering.

The solution is to take something to the marketplace and get feedback.

"Real artists ship." – Steve Jobs

Jobs was referring to the idea that real artists deliver value. They send products into the marketplace. They learn from real users of the product. They improve the product for the next iteration.

To know if you have something people want, see if you can get real customers to let you know what they prefer.

For example, I wanted to give a speech on "pitch hacks." A meeting planner was concerned that the title that I had was not clear enough. I worked with my team and the title became "Pitch with Extreme Confidence: The Pitch Hacking Method."

One of my mentors mentioned taking "imperfect action." We do not wait for the perfect form of some item. For example, I have worked with clients who did not think their biography was "perfect enough yet."

I asked, "Does your biography communicate what you

bring to the table? Is it clear about your credentials and what you can do for the client?"

When the client says "yes," then the biography is "good enough," and the client can use his or her speaker one sheet as a tool for getting speaking engagements. Sure, the client can later revise her biography. Still, she has not let the biography become a roadblock, stopping her from moving forward.

In summary, use the *Power of Three* so you enter the marketplace, create momentum and refine as you go along.

Take action and move forward.

Bonus Material #2

The Secret to Drop Nervousness and Pitch Powerfully

On stage, I shook so badly that my right leg fluttered like a hummingbird's wings. I was stuck. Where? I was stuck in "How am I doing?! How am I doing?!"

When I coach a client to give a great pitch to gain funding, I help the person shift out of such a dis-empowered state. I've been a professional speaker over 16 years, and I know what it takes to shift to the power to perform well.

"We'll have you shift out of 'how am I doing?' into 'how are YOU doing?'" I say to my client.

This means that you prepare so well that you're connected to the investors.

So, leave self-consciousness behind.

Think of it: What does the investor want? To avoid making a mistake. What's the big mistake?—picking someone you can't trust to do what it takes to succeed.

Making a business work requires the flexibility to pivot

fast and the power to stay strong and persist.

Investors test us when we're giving a pitch before them.

Can you take a tough question and keep your poise?

Have you rehearsed more than just the text?

While I work with a client, I say, "Your mind just went blank! Use a Recovery Method."

Recently, I saw Auli'i Cravalho perform "How Far I'll Go" (song from Disney's *Moana*, the animated feature film)—during the Oscars. Several performers behind her, swung huge flags. I thought, "Careful, don't hit—" THUD—one performer hit Auli'i in the head with a flag.

Did Auli'i miss a beat?

No. She kept singing, beautifully. She's a well-trained, thoroughly prepared professional. What a performer!

That's what I want for you. Be that exceptional pitch-deliverer. It's not just practicing the text of your speech. You need to make a real connection.

Auli'i maintained her connection with her audience and with her song.

What does your investor want? Remember, the idea is to connect with "How are YOU doing?"

The investor wants to know:
- It's safe to trust you.
- You are flexible.
- You care about your product, the people you'll serve, and the investors who will take the journey with you.
- You are confident in yourself.

My phrase is: "Confidence is Contagious; Compassion Is the Path."

The idea is that when you shift from the self-consciousness of "How am I doing?" to "How are YOU doing?"—you're going to a place of compassion. This ties in with my description of the Sequence: "Confidence is contagious. Investors pick it up. You build trust. Trust gets funding."

Make that connection. Learn how to recover if your mind goes blank. (See my articles about this at PitchPowerFest.com.)

Shift your thinking from "How am I doing?" to "how are YOU doing?"

Have that conversation with your audience of investors.

Look people in the eye.

Remember, it looks a like a group, but you're really there with the opportunity to connect with individuals.

Someone asks you a tough question, and you'll reply: "I'm glad you brought that up. Your name is? George? George, it looks like that's important to you. Related to that, I want to emphasize …"

As you can see, we're talking about connecting. When you pay attention to individual investors, you shift out of self-consciousness. You create a conversation.

They can feel your trustworthiness.

Often, as I work with clients, I help them express a personal brand of T.H.O.R.: trustworthy, helpful, organized and respectful.

The Powerful Move is to establish yourself as a peer.

Investors do not fund the work of supplicants.

You and your project are "the prize."

Learn to connect and get your funding.

Tom Marcoux

Bonus Material #3

Remove Blocks So You Enjoy Real Success!

"I've not heard that before, would you say that again?" an audience member asked me.

"If you're looking for a good romantic partner find someone who is *kind and flexible*," I emphasized.

When you really want to succeed, **remove the blocks so you are kind and flexible.**

Our thinking needs flexibility. However, our habitual thoughts can constrict our thinking.

I have a metaphor about flexibility: Every day I do exercises to keep my neck and back flexible.

I'm looking to be flexible in my thinking, too—so I study many books. I have the thoughts, research and feelings of a number of people in mind.

The Power of a Flexible Perspective
I've learned that ...
Life can place you into a new chapter at any time.

Still, **you can declare that you are now beginning a new chapter of life.**

Why is this helpful? You are declaring your flexibility. Over the years, I've learned to adapt when life has tossed in a surprising, tough situation.

One of my favorite quotes is:

"In truth, I am a verb." – Steve Chandler

When you think of yourself as a verb, you are free! Other people may look at their past behavior and give themselves a noun or label like "shy person."

Instead, you can change your behavior. As a child, I acted like a shy kid. As an adult, I take courageous action. Then I'm courageous.

Develop Your Flexibility

Nina, one of my clients, said, "I don't take vacations."

Then an opportunity arose, and Nina considered taking a vacation. Upon her taking that vacation, I commented: "You are now a person who takes vacations. Prosperous, calm, and happy people take vacations."

Why is taking a vacation a good idea?

It's about refreshing yourself and keeping yourself flexible. You also get access to your intuition, and then you can come up with *Leap-Up Ideas* that could vastly improve your business.

[By the way, a vacation can be two days. Or you could declare a mini-vacation of "I'm taking the afternoon off."]

Don't block your blessings. Don't let doubt stop you from getting where you want to be. – Jennifer Hudson

Learning to let go should be learned before learning to get. Life should be touched, not strangled. – Ray Bradbury

Remember to cultivate two powerful practices: be kind to yourself and others—and be flexible.

Bonus Material #4

Lead and Succeed

Extreme Confidence in leadership is about your skills to read people and communicate in ways they can hear you. One of my phrases is: "They can't hear you with their ears stuffed with pain."

You might respond, "Wait a minute. People don't always walk around in pain." I hear you. Still, let's pause a moment.

I illustrate this point with my audiences and graduate students. With MBA students at Stanford University, I had a student hold up a hand, palm facing me. I pushed on the student's hand and he pressed back. This illustrated a Natural Resistance.

We have a natural resistance, often to new ideas or a new perception. Where does the pain come in? There is pain involved with admitting that a new way of doing things might be better! That means we did something that was "wrong." It's easier to avoid the discomfort of having one's thoughts shaken up.

The term for the state of mental stress when one's

thoughts are inconsistent and opposing each other is called *cognitive dissonance.* A person experiencing cognitive dissonance feels upset, possibly angry or even a bit lost or confused.

For example, Susan, after living apart from her sister Alana for a few years, flew into the state, and they had dinner. Susan was shocked to hear certain words expressed by Alana. Her experience was one of *cognitive dissonance:* "My sister who has been kind to me and who is intelligent is…a… racist?!"

So, what happens in a case like this? Instead of letting ourselves *feel the discomfort of cognitive dissonance,* **we simply resist.**

On the other hand, the successful leader solves this problem by telling an effective story.

An effective story does two things: a) it gets around natural resistance and b) it avoids creating cognitive dissonance.

When you tell a story, you do not slam the listener with an oppressive opinion. Instead, you take the person on a journey. You give them an experience.

Conventional Approach: **Speak directly using logic to push your vision forward.**

vs.

Extreme Confidence Approach: **Invite them in. Use a story to avoid natural resistance.**

What does it take to tell an effective story?
1) Start with "Who's getting hurt?" This is a quick way to identify the victim. Additionally, you identify the villain as the person or group that creates the problem.
2) Provide suspense by showing how tough the situation

is.
3) Provide the triumphant ending. The listener gets to feel great as they experience the great conclusion to the story.

A story does not have to be elaborate. One can do a natural lead-in to the story. Here's an example: Jackson comes to his supervisor, Mary, with a problem.

"I just can't get the people in Dept. XY on board with the new initiative," Jackson says.

"I hear you. That can be really tough to endure," Mary begins. "This reminds me of how I saw a guy lead some people at the previous company I worked for. Would you like to hear, what he did to turn things around?" Mary asks.

"Sure. I'll take anything now."

And, Mary launches into the story.

Leading is often about connecting your team member to their best skills, energy and output.

We can do that through a story. The story doesn't have to be long.

There are times when I say something as simple as "One of my mentors told me: 'Look for the third alternative.'"

"What's the third alternative?" my team member asks.

"It's when two people have two opposing viewpoints. But they keep talking, and they find a third solution that builds on what they were both talking about."

How can you use a story to lead your team?

Bonus Material #5

Don't Let Fear Kill Your Divine Appointment

"What's a Divine Appointment?" my client, Glen, asked.

"It's a moment and place where you must be present to fulfill your real destiny. Perhaps, you need to take a particular meeting with someone. Or maybe you need to give a speech because you're supposed to meet someone in the audience—just after your speech."

We'll use the D.I.V.I.N.E process:

D – Don't let fear kill your Divine Appointment
I – invest your best in the moment
V – verify what is "pollution"
I – identify the Divine Appointment
N – nurture and prepare
E – energize yourself

1. Don't let fear kill your Divine Appointment
To make it to your Divine Appointment, you might have to put the airfare on your credit card. Many of us are fearful

about going into debt.

It's true that there is good debt and bad debt. Good debt is when you invest in yourself and increase your skills and capabilities. Bad debt is buying stuff (certain toys, gadgets, sound systems and more) before your cash flow can support extravagances.

Still, to make the right connections and get access to certain opportunities, you may need to take appropriate risks and go into appropriate debt.

Here's how you note the differences between intuition and fear:

Voice of Fear: contract, hide, avoid taking a risk

Voice of Intuition: expand, experiment, take an appropriate risk.

2. Invest your best in the moment

I also call this: "Give your best in the moment." To open the door for blessings, we often are called to give something. Every day, I provide great support and listening to a number of people. Some are clients. Others are friends or new acquaintances.

"Doing the best at this moment puts you in the best place for the next moment." - Oprah Winfrey

3. Verify what is "pollution"

My client Susan said, "I always carry this book (on making money) around with me."

"Even when you visit your parents?" I asked.

This was a potential problem because Susan had told me about how her parents were unsupportive of her entrepreneurial pursuits.

"Be careful about what books your parents see that you're reading."

"Why?"

"Because they will bury you in pollution," I began. "They'll try to talk you out of your dreams. You've told me about how they want you to 'be realistic' and to settle and to take a real job. For many of us, working a 40-hour regular job can provide stability while we *still* pursue our dreamwork. And, it's important that we protect ourselves from certain negativity."

Having friends or family pull you down is called "crab mentality." One at a time, crabs can escape a bucket—but NO! they are not allowed to. Why? The other crabs hold them down. Then, they will *all* die.

Authors have suggested "crab mentality" is visible in people who envy others and conspire to hold them down.

Guard yourself against "pollution" that chokes your empowered thinking.

4. Identify the Divine Appointment

I have been fortunate that I've shown up for Divine Appointments. I formed a partnership and directed my first feature film. I teamed up with other business owners and in mastermind groups, we supported each other to enhance our businesses.

A Divine Appointment may involve risk, and it's best that we make sure the fear doesn't shut us down emotionally.

How do you know if a particular opportunity is perfect?

You don't. Still, it's worth checking things out.

"It's either Hell Yes or it's Hell No." – attributed to Cheryl Richardson

If possible, give yourself some space and time to feel your way through—so you can assess whether attending an event is a Divine Appointment for you.

When you talk with a trusted friend about an opportunity, be sure to pay attention to how YOU feel as you talk about the potential opportunity.

To identify the Divine Appointment requires that you get quiet time so you can feel your own intuitive assessment of the situation.

5. Nurture and prepare

One of the most important parts of your life is to keep yourself strong and ready. Several people report: "I should have attended that conference. I should have taken that meeting. I was just too tired at the time." Not good enough! Instead, a number of my clients and I keep a log of our sleep. We do what's necessary to stay strong—and then we can jump at opportunities.

6. Energize yourself

"You can help a thousand, but you can't carry three on your back." – Jim Rohn

Make sure that you take care of your own health and personal energy. Divine Appointments require personal energy and resources (like a plane ticket). Make sure to get the exercise, nutrition and sleep you need—so you're ready to jump at a Divine Appointment.

Bonus Material #6

The Power Paradox for Real Success

"I'm looking for some principle that will help me succeed every time," my new client Alex said.

"I've learned that it tends to be a cluster of principles that help. Not just one," I replied.

Then I shared an idea that occurred to me about an hour before the session.

"Alex, it sounds like it would be good for me to introduce you to this detail: The Power Paradox," I began. "The Power Paradox relates to Control in Business vs. Flow in the Moment. I shorten this to *Control or Flow?*"

Learning to let go should be learned before learning to get. Life should be touched, not strangled. – Ray Bradbury

Think about it. Who do you like to work with—someone who is frantic or someone who is calm?

A man without a smiling face must not open a shop.
– Chinese Proverb

When you're skillful about being rested and calm, you attract more business.

Still, seeking to control the controllable variables in one's business is wise. For example, one of my clients, Harry, was having trouble deciding whether to hire George, a contractor.

First, George was quite skilled in work that Harry needed done quite soon.

However, I could tell: Something was making Harry hesitate.

I asked, "Will this guy make your life easier?"

"No," Harry said, quickly—even surprising himself.

"With the energy you said, 'no,' it sounds like you have your answer," I said.

Hiring George would add layers of complication to Harry's life. George was giving clues: Delays in returning Harry's calls and the slow turnaround of an estimate for the work.

There was something that Harry could control: The decision to avoid hiring George and to continue his search for a trustworthy and skilled contractor.

Have you noticed that some people hate to stay in the "decision making phase"? That is, the tension of no answer really bothers them.

This returns us to *The Power Paradox: Control in business vs. Flow in the Moment ... Control or Flow?*

When you take good care of yourself, you can hold on during the tension-times. You can hear your intuition so that you can make a good decision about *Control or Flow*.

Bonus Material #7

Discover the Turning Point that Massively Improves Your Life

Years ago, Ben, one of my close friends, said that he was a depressed person.

I gently suggested: "You're a spirit that deals with depression symptoms."

That phrase meant nothing to Ben. He had applied the label of "depressed person" to himself. He kept saying, "I am a depressed person."

Over the span of two years, I did *not* press the idea of "deals with depression symptoms" on Ben. I think the idea came up three times.

Then one day, I heard Ben say, **"To deal with my depression symptoms**, I take a walk each day. I especially aim to walk when the sun's out."

Wow!

It's been ten years since that time, and Ben tells me that he feels so much stronger now.

Can changing one's words make a big difference?
This idea rose in my thoughts:

If you say "symptoms", you can do something about it.
If you say an "I am", you're stuck.

Natalie, one of my clients, said, "I just don't have a way with words."

"Maybe that's how things appear at this moment. Would you like to get better with words?" I asked.

"I think so," she said.

"There are a number of small methods, you can try. Would you like to start with a couple of details?"

"Yes."

I shared several details including:

Writers know to capture the words whenever they arrive: upon awakening, while you're eating, while you're showering. Writers do *not* operate under the illusions of "great writers always write well on first try" or "I need to feel like it to start writing."

My point here is that some people apply a disempowering label "not good with words" or "bad at writing."

Instead, we can say something like: "I'm learning more about how to improve my writing."

The Turning Point that Massively Improves Your Life
The Turning Point is when you decide to free yourself of a label and instead become "an explorer." If you have "depression symptoms," you're free to try several things like "take a walk each day."

Researchers have noted that daily exercise works so well. One author noted: "But you cannot put exercise into a pill, so it does not get the media attention that it deserves."

Realize that your choice about your own words and your own labels for yourself Make a Big Difference.

Consider calling yourself a learner, an explorer, a person learning more and more about (some topic).

Take a step. Rise up. Find out that *better and different* ARE possible.

P.S. I'm always taking note of phrases that can help me express myself with more clarity.

In one conversation with a friend, I tinkered with these words:

"You know how you hear a great speech or pitch, and it's like music? I'll help you find *your* music. I'm the Spoken Word Strategist."

My point is: **Writing well includes just capturing words as they arrive.**

Bonus Material #8

Stay Connected with People

"How are things going?" I sent as a chat-message to a Facebook friend.

"That's what I'm trying to figure out," he responded.

Soon we were talking on the phone.

I've learned that simply giving people an opportunity to express their current experience, thoughts and feelings deepens friendships. Friendships also yield surprise opportunities.

Recently, I posted this message:

"How fun! I just replied to a Facebook friend's post related to how much reading she needed to complete. I replied: "I hear you about the reading. I share speed-reading tips with my graduate students/clients. Some tips include: 1) Use your hand (fingers on the page) as you read. 2) move your hand a little faster than is comfortable, 3) do Not go backwards (that is, with your hand on the page you won't go back to the top of the page—which slows down reading) ...

More advanced techniques involve avoid sounding out each word. Realize that the words are "pictures," and your brain is picking things up. I also put a mark at the paragraphs I've read so I don't re-read material. I also use Posted Notes—so I stop when I'm bored at a particular page (I go back to the section later.) ... (I trained MBA students at Stanford University—and as a bonus, the Stanford-leadership gave me a speed-reading course. It's helpful. I read 88 books last year.)"

This above selection of reading tips was shared a number of times on Facebook.

I'm helping people I do not even know yet.

It all began with my wanting to provide some kindness and support to one friend.

How can you demonstrate some kindness and support to individuals as you meet more people?

Bonus Material #9

Confidence is a Toolkit – Now Work It

"I know my material, but my friends say that I just don't look confident when I'm giving a pitch," my client, Abigail, said.

"What do you want in this situation?" I asked.

"I want to look confident. No, I want to feel confident," Abigail said.

"How would you know that you're confident?" I asked.

"I'd feel peaceful," she replied.

"Interesting. I have some ideas that could be truly useful to you. Ready to look at some different ideas?"

"Sure."

"Okay. Imagine that these next ideas I share with you are like some different flowers, blossoming in a garden."

"Okay," Abigail said. Her eyes showed that she was intrigued.

"So, one idea is, 'If I was confident, I'd feel peaceful just before I give a pitch. Here's another idea—like another flower: 'Confidence is NOT comfort.' Now, stay with me. If you use this idea, 'Confidence is NOT comfort,' you FREE yourself," I said.

"How so?"

"You free yourself because you stop waiting for some magic thing to happen to take any discomfort away. More than that, you'll be able to jump in and take positive action. Here's something valuable: *Confidence is a toolkit—now work it.*"

"A toolkit? What's in it?"

"A number of techniques that I've learned in over 16 years as a professional speaker—and as an introvert," I said.

"Yes. We talked about that. We're both introverts," she replied.

"We're going to do some *Effective Rehearsal* today," I began. "It's *not* just about memorizing your text. It's not about raising your hand to gesture on a particular word. Instead, I'll show you how to **Pivot in the Moment.** I'll show you how to read the audience and slide into another technique—into another speech pattern. You could slide into asking a question that engages the audience. Something that wakes them up. Or even a bit of humor," I said.

Abigail was smiling.

"Today, I'm opening up that confidence toolkit. I'm teaching you the techniques of Extreme Confidence," I said.

"How is it extreme?"

"We are rising to the *Extreme Confidence* level when you KNOW that you know how to adapt to anything. I'll show you methods. We'll find which ones really connect with you as an individual. You'll be prepared to deal with tough moments: your mind going blank, an investor asking the WORST question. I'll show you have to maintain your poise and STILL get time to think!" I said. "This is not just about words or memorizing. With *Effective Rehearsal,* the techniques become Part of You. We customize the process. I'll show you. Give me the opening words of your pitch."

"Hello, I'm Abigail. I'm CEO of XY Corp. Today, I'm going to—"

"Pause," I said.

"What?"

"You've just wasted the first 20 seconds of your pitch. I'm going to ask you about what you might prefer here. I'll give you a couple of choices to start with. You could start with a question. You might start with a story. For example, 'Sam steps into his office, and he finds something that he's been dreading—'

Abigail leaned forward.

"You see, I've already got you. You're into the story. Or you could start with a question. I'll show the structure. "What is the XY thing that is doing the TERRIBLE THING to the 123_people?"

Abigail looked concerned. She asked, "Why is it so important to be so particular about the opening sentence?"

"It's the first impression. The audience wants to know if they're going to have endure another amateur. They want to be safe. They want to be in the hands of a pro." I said. "So, Abigail, what feels better to you? Start with a story? Or start with a question?"

"I'd like to try a story first," she replied.

"Great."

* * *

In summary:
- Confidence is NOT comfort.
- Confidence is a toolkit—now work it.
- Extreme Confidence is about practicing techniques

so you can adapt to anything.

** **Special Note:** My online course *Get the Big YES: Use Extreme Confidence to Get Clients and Get It Done!* includes 20 videos and 17 audios as part of the training. Also, students work with partners in the course. (For more information, please send an email to tomsupercoach@gmail.com)

Bonus Material #10

Stop Blocking the Amazing You

One of my speeches is titled: "Stop Blocking the Amazing You." We'll now go behind-the-scenes. At press time, this is a version of the speech. It is my practice to "talk through the speech" so you'll notice that this material is in spoken English:

> "Streetlamps hardly make a dent in the darkness. It's after 9 pm. Telegraph Hill neighborhood, San Francisco. I have no idea that my life is going to be on the line.
> Here's how it began. I'm walking with the love of my life, Johanna.
> How do I know that? I'll tell you. It's 17 years later, and she's here in this audience.
> Johanna and I are walking—when one block away, we hear CRASH. We see a huge Ford F-150 truck that slams into Johanna's *parked*, little Toyota truck.
> This huge truck pulls back and smashes her truck again.
> I go 'knight in shining armor' because I'm concerned for

Johanna—that she's going to be hit by an emotional piano because it's *not* her truck. It's her *parents'* truck. She'll be hit by "What did you do?! How did you let this hit-and-run thing happen?!"

The huge truck is trying to get away.

So, I'm running down the center of the street toward the situation.

She walks down the sidewalk because she's *sane* and rational.

That guy turns his truck, trying to get away and PTAK!—hits me, right in the chest.

I don't know how bad it is. I'm full of adrenaline.

He keeps pushing me with his truck. I end up holding onto the hood; my feet are off the street.

What would you do?

I want to talk about emotion. How emotion gets us into things like this trouble with the truck. And how we can *use* emotion. Because I want to help everyone here to **Stop Blocking the Amazing You.**

The Amazing You is that part of you that is naturally courageous. The Amazing You is FREE to be creative, loving, helpful. The Amazing You makes a contribution to the rise of humankind. I invite you to realize that you have already had glimpses of the Amazing You.

You unleash the Amazing You when you become skillful with emotion.

To unleash the Amazing You, we have two parts.

The first part is to make a better decision in a crisis.

The second part is: you *perform at your best*—day to day.

The center of this is five words: "Better Decisions *during* the Emotion."

I'll share that again: "Better Decisions *during* the Emotion."

I was talking with a friend. I said, "Oh yeah, you'll make decisions in a crisis. Some of those can get you killed!"

You need to become skillful with emotion.

We want you to unleash the Amazing You.

I was *not* skillful with emotion during that night when the truck hit me. Recently, it's 17 years later, I was talking with Johanna. I said, "So, with that truck situation, I did a grand romantic gesture…"

"That was stupid," … she said.

Oh, well …

To unleash the Amazing You, you become skillful with emotion.

I know a lot about emotion because as a kid, growing up … I need to tell you about my father. I love my father. I'm grateful to my father. He helped me get into a good school. He helped me with piano lessons and karate lessons.

Also, I need to share that my father went from being an alcoholic, to stop drinking, *not healing anything*, and straight to a rage-aholic. So, I grew up with my father grabbing me by the hair, lifting me to my feet. He threw me into walls— and spit on me.

You got to know, that as a kid, I cried, because my hair came out on my pillow. I thought I'd grow up and be bald like my father.

But my father cared enough about me to get me those piano lessons and karate lessons.

At the age of 15, I had the muscles and the training, and **I knew my father's abuse of me had to stop.**

I had to **stop the cycle of violence**. My grandfather on my father's side died in a bar fight.

I'm fifteen years old. My father grabs me by the hair again. He pulls me up to my feet. My fist is balled up; I'm on the edge of punching my father right in the mouth. Here's the thing: My father is a former Marine. My father and I fighting means something is going to be broken. His face, my arm, something worse. Because I know the rage in my father.

In that moment, I went calm inside. I didn't punch my father. I made a decision. I punched a hole in the wall.

He said, 'God damn it. Look what you did to the wall!"

But he never lifted me by my hair again. He never spit on me again. He never threw me into another wall.

And I'm wondering. What was it that stopped me from being a victim?

This was a good moment for me. We've all had good moments. **But how could a fifteen-year-old, right in the middle of being attacked, go cool and calm—and NOT punch his father?**

My father did me a favor. He probably didn't know it. When he sent me to each karate class, the instructors had the students meditate. They had us close our eyes. As a nine-year-old kid, I didn't know what that was about.

But I now know: I went to a Quiet Center. When I say a Quiet Center, we're talking about there is a part of you. It's natural. It's in there. You need to access it in a crisis. **Before a crisis, you need practice in accessing this Quiet Center.** I had practice reaching my Quiet Center because of all the karate classes—in which they had us sit there and close our eyes—before class.

Because I could to access my Quiet Center, I could **Stop the Cycle of Violence.** Stop my father from hurting me, anymore.

I am talking about **3 Minutes to Change Your Life.**

This is how you can **Make Better Decisions** *during* **the Emotion.**

3 Minutes for meditation. It begins with *Stop. Breathe. Observe.*

That's what I did at fifteen-years-old. I stopped. Took a breath. And observed that there was a way for me to stop the situation—*without* hitting my father. I made a cool, calm decision to punch a hole in the wall, saying that *This ends now.*

Let's all take in a breath, right now. Breathe in. Hold that. And let it out.

Good!

The idea with meditation is that you're doing breathing—and you get quiet for 3 minutes.

There is a lot of useful data about meditation.

Dr. Emma M. Seppälä of Stanford University emphasizes over ten years of research on the benefits of meditation. Research that shows that we can reduce stress. And we can think clearly.

That brings me back to **Better Decisions** *during* **the Emotion.**

We have more verification of the value, particularly in business.

Harvard Business Review in 2017 ran an article emphasizing a 10-year study known as the CEO Genome Project. The leaders of this study, Elena Botelho and Kim Powell noted this:

- "The CEOs who could think clearly and who excelled at adapting are 6.7 times more likely to succeed.
- The CEO candidates who scored high on reliability were twice as likely to be picked for the role and 15

times more likely to succeed in it."

I'm saying that *reliability*—reliability of your thinking processes—it all starts with 3 Minutes a Day—meditation. **3 minutes to change your life.**

This is the power. Your ability to go to your Quiet Center.

Remember, **Better Decisions** *during* **the Emotion.**

I was able to go to my Quiet Center when I found that my mother had cancer. She was going into a breast cancer operation under local anesthetic. My father, who had the persona of Tough Guy, former Marine, former guy from the Air Force—my father could NOT bring himself to go into the operating room—to hold my mother's hand during that operation under local anesthetic. He couldn't do it. I did see tears in his eyes when he heard my mother had cancer.

But my father could *not* stand by her. I'm the only son. I'm the only kid. No one else would go in that room. And my mother only speaks broken English.

So, I decided I would go into that operating room, with my mother. But I was immediately afraid. Because just a few weeks before that—my girlfriend had gone into the Emergency Room. An intern stabbed her in the arm, trying to set an IV. He made a mistake. Her blood went SPEESHHH out of her arm. I got woozy. I got dizzy.

I found out, if someone I love is bleeding, I might lose consciousness.

I thought if I go in the operating room and see my mom being cut into—her chest cut into—I thought I would throw up into the doctor's mask. But I was going to do it.

Stop. Breathe. Observe. I'm going to be with my mother. I'm going to stand in the place of my father.

Now my father had stood in an important place—he served as a Marine and a time in the Air Force. He stood in the place to help me and other Americans be free.

I'm talking about **Stop Blocking the Amazing You.** We all have a choice. We have a choice to take 3 minutes for meditation—and then we can BE FREE. Free of emotion that can mess us up. Free to use good emotion like love, and do things you've never done before.

So here I go—with my mother—into the operating room. And if I throw up in my mask—then tough. I will be there for my mother. I'm scared. But I hold her hand, and she's scared worse.

They do the local anesthetic. The doctor begins the lumpectomy. My mother's holding my hand. My fingers are going white because she's gripping my hand so tightly. I say to the doctor, 'My Mom needs more local anesthetic please."

He says, "What? Is she in pain?"

I'm thinking: "Yeah, Captain Obvious." But I don't say that out loud.

I say, "Yes, please. She needs more local anesthetic."

He gives her that, and my mom eases up. I know that I was there for my mother when she needed me.

So, let's put this into the context of *Stop Blocking the Amazing You.*

3 Minutes of Meditation is that Tool that you can use to *Stop Blocking the Amazing You.*

What's blocking us? For many of us, it's all about emotion. Emotion can block us—Fear, Upset or Anger. **The Answer is, through meditation, you practice going to Your Quiet Center.** That part of you that is strong. That part of you that is calm. That part of you that leads you to make Better Decisions in a Crisis. ... *Better Decisions during the Emotion.*

We began our conversation by talking about my getting

hit by the truck. I had stopped meditating for years. So, I did NOT have this tool. I didn't have the ability to make the wise decision. One of my friends said, "You know, Tom, you should have just written down the license plate number—instead of putting your body in front of the truck."

You see, because I didn't *Stop, Breathe, Observe*. Because I didn't have years of meditation, I put myself in danger, and I got hit by the truck. I ended up in the Emergency Room, and the doctor is pushing on my chest.

Does that hurt?

Yeah.

Does that hurt?

Yeah.

Does that hurt?

Stop that!

The idea is I lost—because I had stopped meditating—I lost the ability to go to my Quiet Center. Meditation is *not* something that you do once, and it stays with you. Meditation is a daily 3 minutes to change your life.

If you ask me now, 17 years later: Would you get in front of that F-150 Truck? I'd say. No! Dying is not a good plan!

The good plan is to *Stop, Breathe, Observe.* Because you can think better and use emotion better. This is how you can *Stop Blocking the Amazing You.*

Because a lot of us are run by emotion. And some of us are run by negative emotion like my father.

Meditation—as in *3 Minutes to Change Your Life*—can help us become stronger. We can make a shift from negative thoughts and limiting thoughts. If you're upset that your first thoughts about something are negative … Let's blame it on the ancestors. The ancestors who said "Saber-toothed tiger. That's negative. I'm out of here"—those are the ones who lived. Other ancestors who saw a saber-toothed tiger and said, "Hello Kitty." They didn't live. So, they didn't pass on their genes to us.

Being negative for many of us, including myself, can be a default setting.

How do you break that default setting?

3 Minutes to Change Your Life. That's how we *Stop Blocking the Amazing You.*

Many of us won't even try something new. Because we make it too hard. A lot of us have heard: 20 minutes of meditation in the morning and 20 minutes at night. We're not going to do that. I don't do that. We don't have the time.

But then I looked into some research, and it turns out that 3 Minutes really *can* change your life.

It certainly changed my life when I was confronted with that violent situation with my father. **I could make the better decision in a crisis.**

Research shows that if, in three minutes, you focus on one image and one sound—this puts your brain in neutral.

So, I invite everyone, right now to look at something: your ring, a bracelet, or your thumb—and we'll make a sound, the Ahhh sound for just a few seconds. We're not going for 3 minutes right now. We're just going for a few seconds. Remember to look at your bracelet or your thumb. Let's all make the sound: Ahhhhhhhhhhhhh.

Well done!

You can do that for 3 minutes every morning. Or some version of it.

I'm just asking for 3 minutes to change your life.

Now, let me take you to Part Two of releasing the Amazing You.

First, we talked about how to make Better Decisions during a crisis.

Now we need you to **Perform at Your Best**—day to day. This is about **Optimize Your Goals.**

The problem is that many of us emotionally shut down because we're unskillful when setting goals. Some of us set our goals too high, and then we just ignore it. We get too busy.

I saw this happening with my new client, Amanda. She was a project manager, until her mother became ill. One of the last things her mother said was: "I was part of a generation of women who put aside their dreams to focus on only one dream, which was family. And that was good. But you have more opportunities, Amanda. I want something different for you. Do something for yourself. Express yourself."

Amanda made a promise to her mother and to herself that she would start her own business. And she would express herself and help people while doing that. But on a day-to-day basis, she was failing to live up to her promise to her mother.

I had a conversation with her. I asked, "Amanda, how are your marketing phone calls going?"

She says, "They're *not*. I'm just way too busy. I can't do it."

Amanda has a problem. She needs **Better Decisions** *during* **the Emotion.** Her emotion is about the pain she feels connected to making sales calls.

I say, "Amanda, I get it. And, many times, when we say, 'I can't do it,' it means we're in some kind of denial. Or something else. I want to share with you something I've learned: **What you dread, gets you ahead.**

I'll share that again. **What you dread, gets you ahead.**

"So, Amanda, let's make a shift. Let's look at these goals

and focus on *3 Levels of Goals*.

"So, you can *Stop Blocking the Amazing You*. Let's start with the Amazing level. How many marketing phone calls in one day?"

She says, "Fifteen."

"Great. And, what would be a good number?"

"Five."

"Amanda, would you do five?"

She says, "Maybe not."

"Would you do two?"

She says, "Yeah. I could do two in eight hours. Sure."

I say, "Great. We know that Good is two marketing phone calls. We know *Amazing* is fifteen. And we know that anything over two is *Excellent!*"

Good, Excellent, and Amazing.

This is powerful. This is how we can get people to stretch. This is how people can do things they've never done before. This is how to *release the Amazing You*.

This is how I have been able to do many things that have scared me.

Like getting ready to speak in front of 700 people for the first time.

Like directing my first feature film.

I've been able to do those things because of two sets of 3 Minutes.

3 minutes to Change Your Life in terms of meditation.

3 minutes to Optimize Your Goals. That's setting goals on the *Three Levels: Good, Excellent and Amazing.*

For example, when I was terrified to direct my first feature film, I took a moment to *Stop, Breathe and Observe*.

I realized: I'm afraid, but I could prepare. I could do a few storyboards. So, I could really understand this movie. So I'll be prepared. That would be *Good*—a few storyboards.

I ended up personally drawing 801 storyboards. To me, that was *Amazing*.

I was *thoroughly prepared* to direct my first feature film.

That's the point: You use Good, Excellent and Amazing, and you will stretch yourself.

I've also learned that Amazing—in working with my own coach—and when I coach other people ... **Amazing happens with Alliances.**

Yes—*Amazing happens with Alliances.*

You can have a coach. You can team up with other business owners. You can have mastermind groups. *Amazing happens with Alliances.*

When you set Amazing goals, you have something to strive for. It's in front of your eyes. You can get there. You can go forward and stretch yourself.

At the same time, when you set modest Good-level goals, you *avoid* beating yourself up. People beat themselves up because they do *not* set the level of "Good."

You'll have good days.

I strive to the level of excellence. So, I have many Excellent Days.

Let me share that that using *Good-Excellent-and Amazing* functioned like opening a new door for Amanda. She set these goals *Good-Excellent-and Amazing*. That's how she used the process: **Stop Blocking the Amazing You.**

She stopped shutting down emotionally. She raised her sights. She took some action.

In closing, let's pull this all together.

Let's just take a moment and think about own lives.

Wouldn't you like to Amaze yourself?

Stop Blocking the Amazing You.

Remember, the Amazing You is naturally courageous. The Amazing You is FREE to be loving, creative and make a great contribution. The Amazing You contributes to the rise of humankind.

The Amazing You feels ALIVE, fulfilled and happy.

It all comes down to **Two Sets of Three Minutes.** 3 minutes to change your life.

3 minutes of meditation. And three minutes to Optimize Your Goals.

Meditation will make you stronger—so you can do things you've never done before.

You may not have to hold your mother's hand in an operating room. But something in life is coming. Something will challenge you. Something will call on you to be courageous.

You'll need the power of *Stop. Breathe. Observe.*

You'll need to make better decisions in a crisis.

You'll perform better—day to day.

You'll be able to make **Better Decisions** *during* **the Emotion.**

By the way, you'll AVOID putting yourself in front of a truck!

Make sure to make the choice to *unleash the Amazing You!* Thank you."

[*It has been a joy to share with you this version of one of my speeches. May you put the methods into action and turbocharge your life!*]

** During the process, thanks for listening to drafts of this speech to Barry Adamson III, Jon Colton, Brad Carlson, Linda L. Chappo, Ben Gay III, Stacy Diane Horn, David Laster, Johanna E. Mac Leod, Thomas Price, Dave Strand, and Dave Thude. Many blessings to you.

Amazing You

Bonus Material #11

How You Can *Soar with Confidence*

"*Soar with Confidence*—that sounds powerful—even fun," my friend Trina said.

In my speech, "Soar with Confidence," I focus on the F.L.Y. process:

F – focus on evidence and rehearsal
L – leverage your system
Y – yearn for energy

1. Focus on Evidence and Rehearsal

True confidence, that is, the actual experience of confidence is when you *know* that you know. The way to get to that point is through rehearsal.

Through rehearsal you give yourself *evidence* that, if you're preparing a speech, certain words *are* comfortable. These particular words come out of your mouth smoothly.

Some people write a speech. I'd rather *talk my way through* speech writing process. Why? Because I know that the words are natural, and they're flowing from my mouth. I know that I'm comfortable. I know which words may be difficult for me to express. I once practiced for days to say "verisimilitude."

Perhaps, you'd like to say:

"antidisestablishmentarianism"?

The power of rehearsal is that you feel stronger as you improve your speech.

Confidence is not comfort.

But strength can be enhanced. You take action and you develop that strength. In taking action, you're developing the strength of certain neural pathways in your brain. You are laying down the track—these new neural pathways—so your brain naturally goes in a stronger direction. *You create what you really want in life.*

Rehearsal is how you get to the point that you know what you know.

And you keep a Progress Log.

While someone else may postpone rehearsal, *you have evidence* that you are putting in the time. Your Progress Log is the evidence.

On the other hand, Brian Grazer, producer of *Apollo 13* starring Tom Hanks, has revealed that he postpones doing anything on an upcoming speech until two weeks before the speech date. He says that preparing for a speech gives him feelings of being anxious.

Here's another approach. My clients and I deal with anxiety by working on the speech for all the weeks before the speech. I rehearse a little each day—even if it's just 9 minutes a day.

Here's what you get from this form of rehearsal: You gain some certainty of your "instrument," that is, your brain. You know your brain is working with the material. Your voice is working. Your tonality and your body language are working. *That's the power.* And that's the benefit. That's why *focus on evidence and rehearsal* matters.

2. Leverage your system

Why does using a system matter? It matters because a *System is more powerful* than willpower. If you want confidence, then **have systems in place.** In this way, know that you will do what you need to do to excel—to be extraordinary.

With a system of rehearsal, you provide yourself time to think through and feel your way through to a great performance.

The big benefit is: You develop strength and a better performance for when you're in a tough situation. By being well-rehearsed, you actually *free yourself up* to smoothly improvise in the moment.

How will you keep track of your rehearsals? Will you identify 3 to 5 people to rehearse with? Will you engage a coach?

3. Yearn for energy

I've learned that we really need to devote time, as we get older, to renewing your energy. Creating calm energy can help us create the capacity for endurance.

I remember a time I gave a speech with so much exuberant energy that I found myself breathing rapidly. Out of breath. I was shocked. I had to build up my endurance and my capacity to speak with total energy and lots of movement.

To have confidence, to *soar with confidence,* you need to know that you're constantly improving and expanding your capacity. *Yearn for energy* is about increasing your capacity.

Confidence comes from capacity to perform at your best.

Get the Big Yes™

Use *Extreme Confidence* to Get Clients and Get It Done!

6-Week Online Course

- **Experience Real Confidence**
- **Learn to Gain Trust Quickly**
- **Gain Clients Effectively**
- **Rehearse with a Partner – So the Techniques** *Become Part of You*
- **Overcome Procrastination**
- **Let Go of Fear and Nervousness**
- **Handle Tough Moments (even if your mind goes blank)**

Online Course

Tom Marcoux
Spoken Word Strategist
Contact:
TomSuperCoach@gmail.com

A Final Word and the Springboard to Your Dreams

Congratulations on your efforts with this book.

Please consider continuing to work with me through my **executive coaching** (phone and in-person), workshops and keynote addresses. Visit my blogs:

PitchPowerFest.com
GettheBigYES.com
StopBlockingtheAmazingYou.com
YourBodySoulandProsperity.com

Meanwhile, *to get even more value from this book*, take the plans and insights that you created and place them in some form in your calendar or day planner. *Plan and take action.* Return to these pages again and again to reconnect with the material and take your life to higher levels.

The best to you,
Tom

Tom Marcoux
Spoken Word Strategist

Executive Coach—Pitch Coach

Special Offer Just for Readers of this Book:
Contact Tom Marcoux at tomsupercoach@gmail.com for special discounts on **coaching**, books, workshops and presentations. Just mention your experience with this book.

Apply for a Free Consultation – see the video at TomSuperCoach.com/breakthrough

Excerpt from
Darkest Secrets of Persuasion and Seduction Masters: How to Protect Yourself and Turn the Power to Good
by Tom Marcoux, Executive Coach – Spoken Word Strategist
Copyright Tom Marcoux

... Now, I am in my 40's, with gray in my hair, and for 27 years I have been taking action to protect people.

And now is the time for me to protect you with the Countermeasures I reveal in this book.

Every human being needs to be able to break the trance that a Manipulator creates. You need to make good decisions so you are safe and you keep growing—and you are not cut down and crippled.

This Darkest Secrets material is so intense that I first released it only with the counterbalance of my most energizing and uplifting books, *Soar! Nothing Can Stop You This Year* and *Year of Awesome: How You Can Use 12 Success Principles including 10 Seconds to Wealth*.

An interviewer asked me: "Who can be the Manipulator?"

A co-worker, a boss, a salesperson, someone you're dating, and someone you think is a friend.

Now is the time—this very minute—for me to write this book to protect you.

I must speak the truth.

These Darkest Secrets of "persuasion masters" are …

Wait a minute! Let's say it plainly: These are the Darkest Secrets of masters of manipulation. Throughout this book, I will call these people what they are: Manipulators.

Dictionary.com defines "manipulate" as "To influence or manage shrewdly or deviously…. To tamper with or falsify for personal gain."

In this book, we will look on a manipulator as one who deviously influences someone with no concern about that person's well-being, and who causes harm to that person.

Here is the first Darkest Secret:

Darkest Secret #1:
Manipulators Make You Hurt
and Then Offer the Salve.

Manipulators would invite you to go out in the sun for hours and then sell you the salve to soothe your burns. The problem is that we don't notice that this is what they're doing.

For example, you're considering the purchase of a house. A Manipulator asks the question, "So, where would you put your TV?" This question is designed to put you into a trance.

Dictionary.com defines "trance" as "a half-conscious state, seemingly between sleeping and waking, in which ability to function voluntarily may be suspended." Let's condense this: in a trance you may not be able to function freely.

Here is the second Secret:

Darkest Secret #2:
Manipulators Put You into a Trance.

To protect yourself, you must learn to use Countermeasures to Break the Trance.

All the Countermeasures (actions you can take to break the trance) in this book will make you stronger and more capable of protecting yourself.

Now, we'll view the third Secret:

Darkest Secret #3:
Manipulators Care Nothing for You and Human Decency: They'll lie, cheat, and do whatever they need to do so they win—but their charm masks all this.

Let's return to the example of a Manipulator selling you a house. A Manipulator does not pause for an instant to see if you can truly afford the new house. The Manipulator would neglect to mention that you will not only have your mortgage payment of $900. There will be additional costs: home repairs, property tax, water, electricity, homeowner's insurance, and more. The Manipulator only emphasizes what he or she knows you want to hear: "Look! $900 is better than the $1500 you're paying for rent, which is just going down the toilet. And the $900 is an investment."

Let's go back to **Darkest Secret #1:**
Manipulators make you hurt and then offer the salve.

The Manipulator has you feeling good about the solution (salve) and feeling bad about your current life situation.

How? A Manipulator will make you hurt through questions such as:

• What bothers you about paying $1500 a month for rent? (The Manipulator will use a derisive tone when he says the word rent.)

• What is not smart about paying rent on someone else's house instead of investing in your own house?

- How do you feel about your children walking in the neighborhood where you live now?

Do you see how these questions are designed to make you hurt enough so that you'll buy?

An interviewer asked me, "Tom, aren't these good arguments for purchasing a house?"

"What we're looking at is the *intention* of the influencer," I replied. "Let's look at our definition of a manipulator as one who deviously influences someone with no concern about that person's well-being, and who causes harm to that person. If the person truly cannot afford the house, he or she will be harmed by buying it. If the manipulator conceals the truth, the manipulator is doing harm. That's the important difference."

Some friends of mine are ethical and helpful real estate agents who truthfully reveal the whole situation and help the purchaser achieve her own goals.

In this book, we are talking about another type of person; that is, unethical Manipulators.

* * *

In any given moment, we need to remember the tactics Manipulators use. We will focus on the word D.A.R.K. so you can remember details easily and protect yourself from Manipulators.

D — Dangle something for nothing
A — Alert to scarcity
R — Reveal the Desperate Hot Button
K — Keep on pushing buttons

1. Dangle Something for Nothing

What do conmen and conwomen do to seize your attention? They make you think you're getting a "steal."

I recently saw a documentary in which a conman on a street in England showed a toy that looked like it was dancing. This fake product was actually dancing because of a hidden, invisible thread. The conman was dangling something for nothing. The Entranced Buyer thought he was getting something worth $20 for only $5. That was the trick. The Entranced Buyer felt that he was getting $15 extra of value for his $5. What the Buyer really got was something worth nothing. Similarly, I know someone who purchased a copy of a Disney movie from a street vendor in San Francisco. She brought the copy home and it was unwatchable—and the street vendor was never seen again.

An old phrase goes, "A conman cannot con someone who is not looking for something for nothing."

How to Protect Yourself from "Dangle Something for Nothing"

Stop! Get on your cell phone and talk through the "deal" with someone you know who thinks clearly. Go home. Think about it. Do some research on the Internet. Listen to your gut feelings. If the salesman or conman is too insistent, get away from that Manipulator. Get quiet. Have a cup of water. Cool down. Break the Trance!

Break the Trance and Identify the Crucial Detail

Earlier, I mentioned that a Manipulator puts you into a trance. An added problem is that we put ourselves into a trance. For example, as you read this, are you thinking about your right toe? Most likely not (unless you stubbed your toe recently). The point is that we only focus on a tiny percentage of what is going on in our life.

Around fifteen years ago, I caused myself trouble because I put myself into a trance. I discovered that under certain conditions, friendship can make you nearly deaf. Here's how: I was producing a song for a motion picture. A good friend was singing backup in the chorus. Because of our friendship, I wanted him to sound great. I completely missed the Crucial Detail. In this kind of situation, the Crucial Detail is that what truly counts is how the lead singer sounds! I made a song that I could not release. What a waste of time and money! I had put myself into a trance.

In any situation in which the Manipulator is "dangling something for nothing," we often fall into a trance and miss the Crucial Detail. The most important detail is *not* that we're saving money if we order before midnight tonight. What counts is whether the product creates a lasting, crucial benefit in our lives. And is the benefit of the product worth the cost? Some people even program themselves to make mistakes by saying, "I can't pass up a bargain." The bargain is *not* the Crucial Detail.

Secrets to Break the Trance

This is the process of B.R.E.A.K.S. It will help you remember the proven methods to break a trance.

B — Breathe
R — Relax
E — Envision
A — Act on aromas
K — Keep moving
S — Smile

Secret #1: Breathe

Remember Secret #1: Manipulators make you hurt and then offer the salve. The Manipulator wants to put you into a state of being that fills you with a sense of urgency and anxiety. Oh, no! I'm going to miss the sale! Stop this highly vulnerable state. Take a deep breath.

End of Excerpt from ***Darkest Secrets of Persuasion and Seduction Masters: How to Protect Yourself and Turn the***

Power to Good

Purchase your copy of this book (paperback or eBook) at online retailers

See **Free Chapters** of Tom Marcoux's 43 books at http://amzn.to/ZiCTRj

ABOUT THE AUTHOR

You want more and better, right? Imagine fulfilling your Big Dream.

Tom Marcoux can help you—in that he's coached thousands of people: CEOs, small business leaders, graduate students (at Stanford University) speakers, and authors.

Tom is known as an effective **Executive Coach** and **Spoken Word Strategist.**

(and Thought Leader—okay, writing 43 books helped with that!)

** CEOs, Vice-Presidents, Other Executives, Small Business Leaders:

You know that leading people and speaking at your best can be tough.

Tom solves problems while helping you amplify *your own Charisma, Confidence, and Control of Time.*

> "Tom Marcoux coached me to get more done in 10 days than other coaches in 2 years."
> – Brad Carlson, CEO of MindStrong LLC

Interested? Email Tom at tomsupercoach@gmail.com Ask for a Special Report: "9 Deadly Mistakes to Avoid for Your Next Speech."

You've heard that you need to tell YOUR STORY well, right? (We're talking about brand, product, or profile for a job.)

The San Francisco Examiner designated Tom Marcoux as "The Personal Branding Instructor." Why? Tom has helped thousands of clients, audiences, MBA students express their own **powerful Personal Brand.** Tom helps **you communicate powerfully so people trust you** and gain what you're offering (product, service, an idea!).

As a **Pitch Coach,** Marcoux is an expert on STORY. He won a Special Award at the EMMY AWARDS, and he directed a feature film that went to the CANNES FILM MARKET and earned international distribution. Tom founded PitchPowerFest.com (Also see GettheBigYES.com)

You need to give a great Speech. How about a TED Talk?

"Tom Marcoux has coached me to make my speeches compelling and powerful. He's helping me prepare my TED Talk. Do your career a big favor and engage **Tom Marcoux, the Spoken Word Strategist.**" – Dr. JoAnn Dahlkoetter, author of *Your Performing Edge* and Coach to CEOs and Olympic Gold Medalists

"Tom helped me unearth deeply emotional and humorous moments in my speech to move the hearts of the audience. He was there for me unconditionally. He went above and beyond anything that I expected. During every interaction that I had with Tom, I felt that I learnt something profound.

I highly recommend for anyone who wants to give a great speech that you work with Tom Marcoux as your Speech Coach and Spoken Word Strategist." – Krishna Noru

As a CEO, Tom leads teams in the United Kingdom, India and the USA. Tom guides clients and audiences (LinkedIn, IBM, Sun Microsystems, etc.) in "Soar with Confidence", leadership, team-building, power time management and branding.

> "Tom Marcoux has been an NAB Conference favorite [speaker] for six years. And he is very energetic." – John Marino, Vice President, National Association of Broadcasters, Washington, D.C.

One of Tom's *Darkest Secrets* books rose to **#1 on Amazon.com Hot New Releases in Business Life** (and in Business Communication). A member of the National Speakers Association for over 15 years, Tom is a professional coach and guest expert on TV, radio, and print.

Tom addressed National Association of Broadcasters' Conference six years in a row. With a degree in psychology, he has presented as a guest lecturer at Stanford University, DeAnza College, and California State University. Over the years, Tom has taught business communication, designing careers, public speaking, science fiction cinema/literature and comparative religion at Academy of Art University. He is engaged in book/film projects *Crystal Pegasus* (children's graphic novel) and *Jack AngelSword* (thriller-fantasy).

This is YOUR OPPORTUNITY. Apply for a <u>Free Consultation</u> with Tom Marcoux at tomsupercoach.com/breakthrough. See the Video.

Tom Marcoux says, "Because of my unique coaching methods, I emphasize with my clients: **You will achieve <u>more</u> than you believe.**"

Tom provides *A.C.T. Coaching* (Assess, Create, Trim) and

T.O.P. Coaching (Transform, Optimize, Power-communicate).

With his unique background as a trained feature film director, actor and screenwriter, Tom will role-play with you so you're ready for the tough meeting and even tougher speech or sales presentation.

> "Using just one of Tom Marcoux's methods, I got more done in 2 weeks than in 6 months." – Jaclyn Freitas, M.A.

Consider Tom Marcoux's **Soar with Confidence Online Course** ... at SoarwithConfidence.com

Become a fan of Tom's graphic novels/feature films:

- Fantasy Thriller: *Jack AngelSword*
  type "JackAngelSword" at Facebook.com

- YA Fiction: *Jenalee Storm*
  At Facebook.com type: "JenaleeStorm"

- Science fiction: *TimePulse*
  www.facebook.com/timepulsegraphicnovel

- Children's Fantasy: *Crystal Pegasus*
  www.facebook.com/crystalpegasusandrose

See **Free Chapters** of Tom Marcoux's 43 books—visible at online retailers.

www.ingramcontent.com/pod-product-compliance
Lightning Source LLC
Chambersburg PA
CBHW070454100426
42743CB00010B/1620